JAPANESE KANA WORKBOOK

JAPANESE

KANA WORKBOOK

by P. G. O'Neill

KODANSHA INTERNATIONAL
Tokyo•New York•London

Distributed in the United States by Kodansha America, Inc., 114 Fifth
Avenue, New York, N.Y. 10011, and in the United Kingdom and con-
tinental Europe by Kodansha Europe Ltd., Gillingham House, 38-44
Gillingham Street, London SW1V 1HU. Published by Kodansha Interna-
tional Ltd., 17-14 Otowa 1-chome, Bunkyo-ku, Tokyo 112, and Kodansha
America, Inc. Copyright © 1967 by Kodansha International Ltd. All
rights reserved. Printed in Japan.

LCC 69-11818
ISBN 0-87011-039-X
ISBN 4-7700-0038-3 (in Japan)

First edition, 1967
92 93 94 95 96 30 29 28 27 26 25 24

CONTENTS

PREFACE

The Japanese *kana* signs are so basic and elementary a part of Japanese writing that the problem they can pose for the beginner is often overlooked. They form a first barrier to the reading of Japanese script which is usually more difficult for the student than it need be.

When learned as isolated elements, the 100 or so *kana* signs require a considerable application of time and unaided visual memory, and peculiarities of their usage are then met only by chance in the later reading of texts; and if the signs and their combinations are learned from their chance appearances in ordinary Japanese texts, it can be a long time before the less common of them are seen often enough to become familiar. In either case, the signs can present problems of recognition and usage long after the elementary stage of the language has been passed in other respects.

This course has been designed to give the student a systematic introduction to the signs and their usage in modern Japanese, without the help of a teacher. Each *kana* is introduced separately and then met in a number of combinations with other *kana* already learned, to build up a cumulative familiarity with the signs. This is tested at intervals throughout the course to show any relearning that might be needed. If this is done, by the end of the course the student will be able to read and write correctly all the *kana* signs and the combinations of them used in the modern writing system.

I should like to thank all those who helped to develop the course by working through preliminary drafts of it, and to acknowledge a particular debt to the publishers, for they have been unsparing in their efforts to make a difficult and laborious production as satisfactory as possible.

P. G. O'Neill

Tokyo, 1967

SPECIFICATION

TYPE OF PROGRAM: A linear program of 1,092 frames. Constructed responses are required throughout, except for a few multiple-choice questions used mainly to test discrimination between *kana* which tend to be confused.

OBJECTIVE: To teach students to read and write the approximately 100 *kana* and the miscellaneous signs associated with them, and to understand and reproduce correctly their usages in modern written Japanese.

TARGET POPULATION: Students in the early stages of their course. Although some little knowledge of elementary Japanese is an advantage, no understanding of the language is necessary for this course.

CONTENT OF PROGRAM: The two groups of *kana* are presented in their usual (*a, i, u, e, o*) order, since students need to learn this to use Japanese dictionaries and other reference works; but the material used to teach the signs differs according to the type of *kana* (see below).

A *kana* is first introduced in copying frames. The main task being the memorization of paired associates (i.e., each *kana* and its sound), the student then goes on to romanize and write it in words where it is used with other *kana* already learned. When a word is to be romanized from *kana*, its meaning is given only after the response, to ensure that students who know the word already do not unconsciously "translate" the meaning instead of reading the *kana*. An average of 10 frames is devoted to each *kana* on its first appearance, after which it reappears irregularly in combination with later *kana*.

> *Hiragana:* To lessen the distraction of new words, vocabulary is restricted as far as possible in this section, and students are advised not to make any conscious effort to learn the meanings of unfamiliar words.
>
> *Katakana:* Since this type of *kana* is used mainly to write foreign (mostly English) loan-words and these words are used for many of the examples, a less restricted vocabulary is used here. Students are required, as before, to romanize words written in *kana*; but when words other than loan-words are required to be written in *katakana*, they are generally given in their *hiragana* forms only (instead of in romanized forms), to

help retention of the *hiragana* already learned. As a check, the romanization is added to the response.

The final part of this *katakana* section deals with certain peculiarities in the Japanese writing of foreign words.

TESTING: Testing and review sections are given at the beginning and end of each main section, to show if any *kana* need relearning. There is a final test involving 246 *kana* units, for which results with 10 or less different mistakes can be considered satisfactory. No retention test has been given, since students are expected to go on to the reading of Japanese texts immediately after finishing the course.

TIME REQUIRED: 10–15 hours for the course itself, apart from relearning time. In testing, the total time required was some 12–20 hours, depending on the time needed for relearning *kana*.

Until students have learned which differences in *kana* forms are significant and which are not, they are often confused by even slight variations. To overcome this, one standard handwritten form has been used throughout this course, and standard printed forms have been given in Appendix 5 for the student to refer to for comparison when he has completed the course.

INSTRUCTIONS FOR USE

1. Cover up the page so that only one numbered frame is visible.
2. Complete the frame as appropriate, usually by writing in the space provided a missing word or *kana* (see "Miscellaneous Signs" below).
3. Uncover the next frame and check your answer with that given in the box to the right of the new frame. Mark with a cross if wrong.
4. Continue as before by answering the new frame.

Do not attempt to learn more than one section dealing with new *kana* signs in any one day. On the other hand, do not leave the course for more than a day or two unless you intend to review the signs already met.

MISCELLANEOUS SIGNS

  indicates a missing letter for each dash
indicates a missing word or words
indicates a missing *kana* sign for each square

I. GENERAL

1	Japanese is normally written in a mixture of Chinese characters and phonetic signs called *kana*. Japanese writing consists of ch_____ and __ __ __ __.	
2	Characters are used in both Japanese and, of course, _____,	characters; *kana*
3	but *kana* is peculiar to_____.	Chinese
4	To write MEANINGFUL words, the early Japanese could use Chinese characters without special difficulty. They simply chose characters with the m_____gs they wanted.	Japanese
5	They could express in writing the idea of "tree" or "heat," for example, by using Chinese characters which had those _____.	meanings
6	Having chosen a character to show the MEANING they wanted, they could then PRONOUNCE it in one of two ways. They had a choice of readings for the s___m___ character.	meanings
7	They could either imitate the Chinese reading for the character, or they could use their own native J_____ word with the appropriate meaning.	same
8	But to write things which were not simple meaningful words (Japanese names, verb and adjective endings, etc.), they often had to ignore the meanings of Chinese characters and use them phonetically. The early Japanese also had to use characters to represent s_____ds.	Japanese
9	When they had no other means of writing, the Japanese had to use characters to spell out much of their language syllable by syllable. This meant writing a character for every such sy_____	sounds
10	Since this was very laborious, simplified forms of characters were developed for this purpose.	syllable

	Syllabic sounds came to be written with _____ forms of _____.	
11	These simplified forms of characters used for their sounds were called *kana*. *Kana* are phonetic signs evolved from _____.	simplified; characters
12	There are two types of *kana*, the first being known as *hiragana*. One type of *kana* is called _____.	characters
13	*Hiragana* means "level/flat *kana*." This name was used because the signs are complete characters "levelled" or smoothed out by being written in running hand. *Hiragana* are the cursive forms of com _____ ch _____.	hiragana
14	The Chinese character 加 with the reading KA, for example, appears in its cursive form か as the *hiragana* sign for *ka*. Similarly, the Chinese character 奈 with the reading NA appears in its cursive form な as the *hiragana* sign for _____.	complete characters
15	*Katakana* is the name of the other type of *kana*. The second type of *kana* is called _____.	*na*
16	*Katakana*, meaning "side *kana*," was so called because each sign consists of only a part, often the side, of a character. *Katakana* were made by using only _____ of a character.	*katakana*
17	The Chinese character 加 with the reading KA, for example, had its left-hand side taken for the *katakana* sign 力 , read _____.	part
18	Similarly, the Chinese character 奈 , with the reading NA, had its top left part taken as the *katakana* sign ナ , read _____.	*ka*
19	Thus, *hiragana* (hereafter abbreviated to H) are smooth, flowing forms of co _____ ch _____ ,	*na*
20	and *katakana* (hereafter abbreviated to K) are stiff, angular p _____ ts of characters.	complete characters

21	Because of this connection with original Chinese characters, and to help the appearance of your own *kana* writing, the correct order of strokes must be followed when learning *kana*. It is important to learn to write *kana* c____ctly.	parts
22	Both H and K contain all the signs needed to represent the sounds used in Japanese. Any Japanese sound can be written in either ____ or ____.	correctly
23	In practice, however, H and K are used differently. Most ordinary written Japanese uses H as the basic *kana*. The main *kana* used in written Japanese generally is ____.	H; K
24	Ordinary written Japanese will also use K for special purposes such as the transcription of foreign words and foreign names not written in Chinese characters. Western words, etc. are written in ____.	H
25	Thus, the *kana* used in books, letters, newspapers, etc. is mostly the soft, cursive ____ with some ____ for special words.	K
26	But the *kana* used for formal, official purposes (e.g. proclamations, military orders) or when clarity is especially important (e.g. telegrams), is usually the stiff, business-like ____ alone.	H; K
27	Most Japanese writing, then, requires a knowledge of both ____ and ____.	K
28	This course deals with H first, and then makes use of these signs to introduce K. It is therefore necessary to work through the course in this order, learning first ____ and then ____.	H; K
29	Japanese is normally written from top to bottom in columns running from right to left. Japanese writing usually starts at the t____ r____ of the page and finishes at the ____ ____.	H; K
30	Sometimes, particularly if many romanized words or mathematical formulae are in the text, Japanese is written from ____ to ____ like English.	top right; bottom left

31	Both kinds of writing allow each *kana* (and Chinese character etc.) the same space in the text, regardless of its shape or complexity. Japanese is written and printed as if every symbol takes up the sa‾_____ sp_____,	left; right
32	and is written with breaks only for punctuation marks. Thus, there are normally no sp _____ between words.	same space
33	Hence, the reader's knowledge of Japanese is the only guide to the div_____n of a text into words.	spaces
34	The basic sounds of Japanese which the *kana* represent are traditionally called the *gozyuu-on* (*gojuu-on*), "the 50 sounds." Learning *kana* consists mainly of learning the H and K signs for these go _____.	division
35	Each type of *kana* has, in fact, only 46 basic signs in general use today and two others seldom used after 1947. In spite of the name *gozyuu-on*, Japanese now uses less than _____ *kana* signs of each type.	*gozyuu-on*
36	These basic sounds and signs are regularly arranged in a special order which is widely used in Japanese dictionaries and reference works of all kinds. It is therefore very necessary to remember the *go* _____ order.	50
37	First come five vowels pronounced, as in Spanish or Italian, roughly like: *a* in "P*a*" (but short) *i* in "(Grand) Pr*i*x" or "p*i*zza" (but short) *u* in "tr*u*e" (but short) *e* in "p*e*t" and *o* in "p*o*rt" (but short) If you are not already familiar with these sounds in this order, repeat them until you can remember them in the correct sequence, PRONOUNCING THEM AS IN THE EXAMPLES ABOVE.	*gozyuu-on*
38	These five Japanese vowels are romanized as *a, i, u, e, o*. Write them out in their correct order, pronouncing them to yourself as you do so: ___, ___, ___, ___, ___.	

39	Next, these five vowels in this same order are preceded by nine consonants in turn, beginning with *k*. Thus, the five sounds which come after the vowels themselves are *ka*, *ki*, _____, _____, _____.	*a, i, u, e, o*
40	The order of the nine consonants is *k, s, t, n, h, m, y, r* and *w*. Complete and learn the following sentence, because the nine consonants in question are the initial letters of its main words and come in the same order: "*Kana* *Signs*: *Take* *Note* __ow__ uch__ ou__ ead and __rite them."	*ku, ke, ko*
41	The nine consonants in their correct order are __, __, __, __, __, __, __, __ and __.	*H, M, Y, R, W*
42	The *gozyuu-on* order of Japanese sounds, then, consists basically of the FIVE vowels __, __, __, __, __,	*k, s, t, n, h, m, y, r; w*
43	and then these five vowels preceded by the NINE consonants __, __, __, __, __, __, __, __ and __.	*a, i, u, e, o*
44	A few sounds (and consequently *kana* signs) are missing, however. Since there have never been combinations of *y + i* or *y + e*, the *y* line has only *ya*, __ __ and __ __,	*k, s, t, n, h, m, y, r, w*
45	and since there has never been the combination of *w + u*, the *w* line consists of *wa*, __ __, __ __ and __ __.	*yu; yo*
46	The initial *w* in this line of *wa, wi, we, wo* is now pronounced only in *wa*. It is therefore useful to show this by putting the other three *w* in brackets and writing the line *wa*, (*w*)*i*, _____. _____.	*wi, we, wo*
47	Also, the *kana* signs for (*w*)*i* and (*w*)*e* are seldom used in postwar writing. You will rarely need to write (*w*)*i* or (*w*)*e*, but you should still learn to rec _____ ze them, because you will meet them in older writing.	(*w*)*e*, (*w*)*o*

48			recognize

There is, however, one other sound and sign.

Since Japanese has one consonant (*n*) which can exist without a following vowel (e.g. *za*N*ne*N), there is a separate *kana* sign for this lone consonant ___.

The complete table of sounds therefore looks like this (a modified *kunreisiki* type of romanization has been used in this course since this is the one most widely used at the elementary level; but variant spellings in the Hepburn-type romanization have also been given in brackets on their first appearance).

n

Vowels:	*a*	*i*	*u*	*e*	*o*
K :	*ka*	*ki*	*ku*	*ke*	*ko*
S :	*sa*	*si* (*shi*)	*su*	*se*	*so*
T :	*ta*	*ti* (*chi*)	*tu* (*tsu*)	*te*	*to*
N :	*na*	*ni*	*nu*	*ne*	*no*
H :	*ha*	*hi*	*hu* (*fu*)	*he*	*ho*
M :	*ma*	*mi*	*mu*	*me*	*mo*
Y :	*ya*		*yu*		*yo*
R :	*ra*	*ri*	*ru*	*re*	*ro*
W :	*wa*	(*w*)*i*		(*w*)*e*	(*w*)*o*
and	*n*				

Both H and K have a separate sign for each of these basic sounds, and the main part of this course will be concerned to help you to learn these two sets of signs.

We have seen that the reader's knowledge of Japanese is the only guide to the division of a text into words. Because of this, count your answers in the following sections right if you have romanized the *kana* examples correctly, even if you have divided the words wrongly.

Also, do not spend time learning or supplying the meanings of the words used as examples. They are given so that you may note—and perhaps remember—them in passing, but your aim here should be solely to learn the *kana* signs and their usage.

II. THE BASIC SIGNS *a* to *ko*   A. HIRAGANA

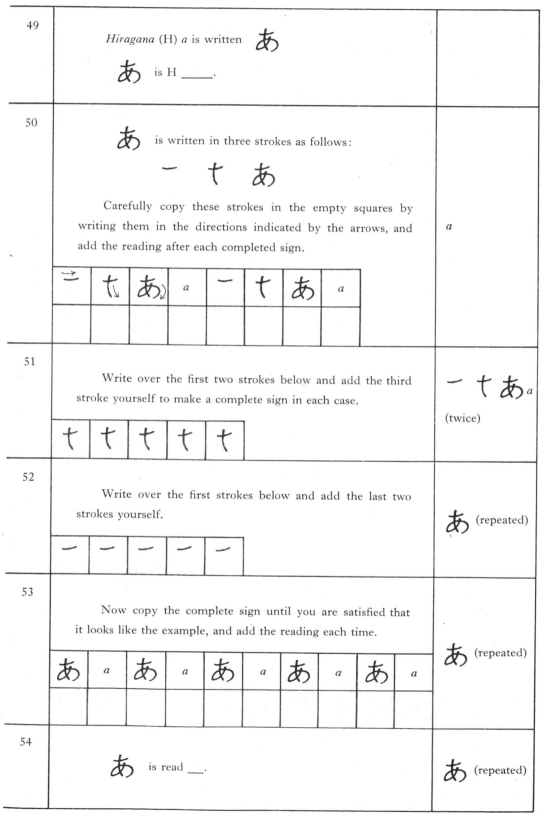

49	*Hiragana* (H) *a* is written あ あ is H _____.	
50	あ is written in three strokes as follows: ー　ナ　あ Carefully copy these strokes in the empty squares by writing them in the directions indicated by the arrows, and add the reading after each completed sign.	*a*
51	Write over the first two strokes below and add the third stroke yourself to make a complete sign in each case.	ー　ナ　あ *a* (twice)
52	Write over the first strokes below and add the last two strokes yourself.	あ (repeated)
53	Now copy the complete sign until you are satisfied that it looks like the example, and add the reading each time.	あ (repeated)
54	あ is read ___.	あ (repeated)

55	H *a* is written		*a*
56	H *i* is written　　い い　is ＿＿ ＿＿.		あ
57	い　is written in two strokes:　　ヽ　い Carefully copy these strokes and the reading in the empty squares.		H; *i*

い　ヽ `i`　ヽ　い　`i`　ヽ　い　`i`

58	Now copy the complete sign until you are satisfied with your writing of it. い　い　い		ヽ　い *i* (repeated)
59	い　is read ＿＿＿.		い (repeated)
60	H *i* is written		*i*
61	あ い　　is read ＿＿＿.		い
62	*Ai* "love" is written		*ai* ("love")
63	After *a* and *i*, the next sound is ＿＿＿.		あ い

64	H *u* is written う , in two strokes: ` う Copy these strokes:	*u*

	う	` う	` う	` う	

65	Now write the complete sign and its reading until you are satisfied.	` う (repeated)

	う	*u*	う	*u*	う	*u*			

66	If う is read ____,	う (repeated)
67	then あう is read ____.	*u*
68	If *u* is written		*au* ("to meet")
69	then *au* "to meet" is written			う
70	Since い is __ and う is *u*,	あう
71	い う can be read *iu*; but when this combination is the verb "to say," it is usually romanized as *yuu*. Thus, *yuu* "to say" is written		*i*
72	The next sound, ____, is written え	いう
73	Copy the two strokes of え and its reading:	*e*

	え	*e*	` え	*e*	` え	*e*		

74	and now the complete sign:	` え *e* (repeated)

	え								

75	え is read __.				え (repeated)
76	Thus, *e* "picture" can be written				*e*
77	but the particle *e* "to(wards)" c_____t be written in this way.				え
78	The particle *e* is always written with an_____er *kana* we shall meet later.				cannot
79	Normally, however, the sound *e* is written		⊠		another
80	*Ue* "upper part, top," for example, is written				え
81	The last of the single vowels, __, is written in H as お				うえ
82	お is read __.				*o*

83	Copy its three strokes carefully, and add the reading.	

⼸	お	お゛	*o*	ー	お	お	*o*		*o*

84	Now practice writing the complete sign:	ー お お *o*

お	お	お					(repeated)

85	あ is read __, but お is read __.		お (repeated)
86	If your answer to the above frame was right, jump to Frame 89. Which is the sign for *a*, お or あ ?		*a; o*
87	What is the other sign お ?		あ
88	H *o* is written	, and *a*	*o*
89	Thus, あ お い is read _____,		お ; あ
90	and お う is read _____.		*aoi* ("blue, green")

No.	Prompt				Answer
91	Conversely, *ou* "to pursue" is written			✕	*ou* ("to pursue")
92	and *aoi* "blue, green" is written			✕	おう
93	We saw that the sign for *e* was not used for the particle *e*. Similarly, the sign for *o* is __ __ __ used to write the particle *o*.				あおい
94	The sound *o* is normally written		in H,		not
95	but NOT when it is the accusative p_____e.				お
96	Hence, none of the five vowel signs is used to write _____.				particle
97	These same five vowels in the same order as above are now preceded by the first initial consonant in the syllabary, _____.				particles
98	This gives the next five sounds: _____.				*k*
99	The first of these, *ka*, is written か か is read _____.				*ka, ki, ku, ke, ko*
100	Copy the following strokes and reading: つ カ か *ka* つ カ か *ka*				*ka*
101	and now the complete sign until you are satisfied: か か か				つ カ か *ka* (repeated)
102	あかい is read _____.				か (repeated)
103	おか is read _____.				*akai* ("red")

#		Answer
104	Kao "face" is written	oka ("hill")
105	Kai "meeting" is written	かお
106	Kau "to buy" is written	かい
107	The sound ki is written き き is the H sign for _____ .	かう
108	Copy the following: ア ミ キ き ki 　ー ニ キ き ki	ki
109	Now practice writing the complete sign: き ki き ki き ki	ー ニ キ き ki (repeated)
110	Ki "tree" is written	き ki (repeated)
111	Kaki "oyster" is written	き
112	お き is read _____ .	かき
113	え き is read _____ .	oki ("open sea")
114	Aki "autumn" is written	eki ("station")
115	Kika "naturalization" is written	あき
116	き is followed by く , the sign for the next sound _____ .	きか
117	Copy its single stroke and reading until you are satisfied with your writing of the sign. く ku く ku く ku	ku

118	*Aku* "to become open" is written				*ku* (repeated)
119	*Iku* "to go" is written				あ く
120	*Uku* "to float" is written				い く
121	か く is read _____.				う く
122	き く is read _____.				*kaku* ("to write")
123	The sign for *ke* is け . Practice writing it in the usual way: い ド け↓ *ke* け *ke*				*kiku* ("to hear")
124	き け is the brusque imperative _____.			い─け *ke* (etc.)
125	か け is the brusque imperative _____.				*kike* ("listen!")
126	*Ike* "pond" is written				*kake* ("write!")
127	*Oke* "tub" is written				い け
128	*Ko* is written こ . Practice it carefully. こ *ko* こ *ko*			お け
129	Thus, *koko* "here" is written				こ *ko* (repeated)
130	but い い is ____.				こ こ
131	*Koe* "voice" is written				*ii* ("good")
132	こ い is read _____.				こ え
133	こ う is read _____.				*koi* ("love; carp")
134	*Koke* "moss" is written				*kou* ("to request")

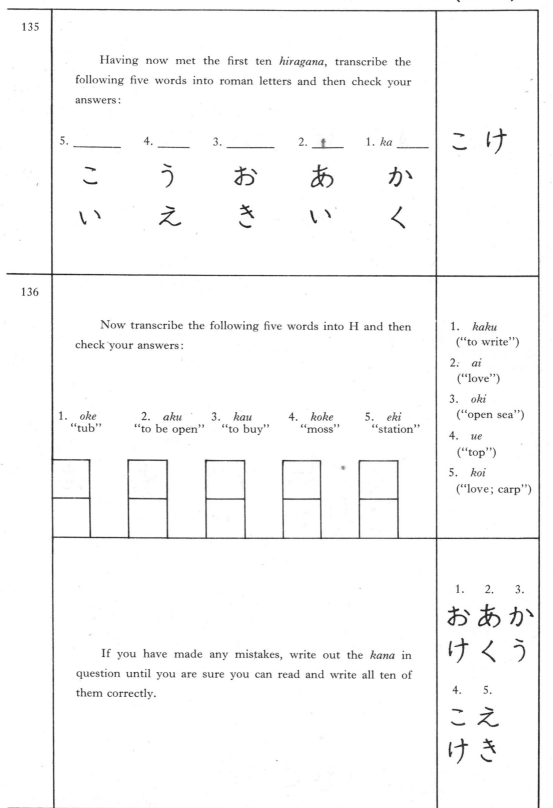

135	Having now met the first ten *hiragana*, transcribe the following five words into roman letters and then check your answers: 5. ____ 4. ___ 3. ____ 2. _ 1. *ka* ___ こ う お あ か い え き い く	こけ

136	Now transcribe the following five words into H and then check your answers: 1. *oke* 2. *aku* 3. *kau* 4. *koke* 5. *eki* "tub" "to be open" "to buy" "moss" "station"	1. *kaku* ("to write") 2. *ai* ("love") 3. *oki* ("open sea") 4. *ue* ("top") 5. *koi* ("love; carp")

	If you have made any mistakes, write out the *kana* in question until you are sure you can read and write all ten of them correctly.	1. おけ 2. あく 3. かう 4. こけ 5. えき

III. THE BASIC SIGNS : *sa* to *to*

Before going on to the new signs in this section, make sure you remember those already met by writing them below.

When you have finished all ten, check with the answers given immediately below and relearn any signs you have wrong. (The *kana* dealt with are shown at the top of each page.)

1. *u*		2. *ki*		3. *a*		4. *ko*		5. *e*	
6. *ka*		7. *o*		8. *ku*		9. *i*		10. *ke*	

1. う 2. き 3. あ 4. こ 5. え

6. か 7. お 8. く 9. い 10. け

137	The next consonant after *k* is ___,	`
138	and the first sound beginning with *s* is _____.	*s*
139	*Sa* is written さ . Copy and practice this.	*sa*

一	さ	さ	*sa*	さ	*sa*

28

140	Distinguish this from き, which is _____.	ー ナ さ *sa* etc.
141	Thus, *ki* is written き, but *Sa* has only a Single cross-stroke and is written [ ]	*ki*
142	く さ is read _____.	さ
143	*Asa* "morning; flax, hemp" is written	*kusa* ("grass")
144	*Sao* "pole" is written	あ さ
145	*Saki* "(pointed) end, tip" is written	さ お
146	*Sake* "rice wine" is written	さ き
147	The next sound, *si* (*shi*), is written し . Practice it as below. し | *si*	さ け
148	Thus, *usi* "cow, bull" is written	し *si* (etc.)
149	*Asi* "foot, leg" is written	う し
150	い し is read _____.	あ し

#							Answer
151	*Kosi* "waist" is written						*isi* ("stone")
152	かし is read _____.						こし
153	*Sika* "deer" is written						*kasi* ("cake")
154	*Sio* "salt" is written						しか
155	*Su* is written す . Copy and practice this:						しお
156	*Isu* "chair" is written						す *su* (repeated)
157	おす is read _____.						いす
158	*Kikasu* "to cause to hear, to tell" is written						*osu* ("to push")
159	*Suki* "like" is written						きかす
160	*Ikasu* "to let live, to revive" is written						すき
161	すし is read _____.						いかす
162	*Sasu* "to point at, to sting" is written						*susi* ("rice-cake")
163	*Kesu* "to extinguish" is written						さす
164	*Sue* "end, the close" is written						けす
165	Usually the honorific prefix *o-* is used with *susi* "rice-cake"; this makes *o-susi*, written						すえ

166	After す comes *se*, written せ Practice writing it:									おすし
	⁻	ナ゙	せ	*se*	一	ナ	せ	*se*		

167	Now practice the whole sign as much as necessary:									一 ナ せ
	せ	*se*	せ	*se*	せ	*se*				*se* (twice)

168	H *se* is written			せ *se* (repeated)

169	せ き is read _____.	せ

170	*Ase* "sweat" is written				*seki* ("seat")

171	*Kuse* "habit" is written				あ せ

172	The place-name *Ise* could be written			✕	く せ

173	The sound after *se* and the last with an initial *s* is ____.	い せ

174	H *so* is written そ . Copy the following:									
	⁋	そ	*so*	ゾ	そ	*so*	そ	*so*		*so*

175	そ こ is read _____.	ゾ そ *so* (etc.)

176	そ し き is read _____.	*soko* ("there")

177	*Asoko* "(over) there" is written			✕	*sosiki* ("system")

#									Answer
178	*Uso* "lie" is written								あそこ
179	After sounds beginning with *s* come those beginning with ___,								うそ
180	and the first of these is ___ .								*t*
181	H *ta* is written た た is read ___ .								*ta*
182	Practice the writing as usual: ⇁ ナ ナ⇁ た〳 *ta* た *ta* た *ta*								*ta*
183	た か い is read _____ .								‐ ナ ナ た *ta* (etc.)
184	き た is read _____ .								*takai* ("high")
185	*Katai* "hard" is written								*kita* ("north")
186	*Taki* "waterfall" is written								かたい
187	*Atatakai* "warm" is written								たき
188	*Itai* "painful" is written								あたたかい
189	*Sita* "lower part; tongue" is written								いたい
190	*Uta* "song" is written								した
191	H *ti* (chi) is written ち . Copy and practice: ⇁ ち〵 *ti* ち *ti* ち *ti*								うた
192	*Titi* "father" is written								‐ ち *ti* (etc.)
193	く ち is read _____ .								ちち
194	*Uti* "home" is written								*kuti* ("mouth")

#	Content						Answer
195	*Iti* "one" is written						うち
196	*Kati* "victory; value" is written						いち
197	ちいさい is read _____ .						かち
198	Thus, *ti* is written ___ , and *sa* is written						*tiisai* ("small")
199	*Tiisai* "small" is written					✕	ち ; さ
200	きち is read _____ .						ちいさい
201	Thus, *ki* is written ___ , and *ti* is written						*kiti* ("good fortune")
202	*Kiti* "good fortune" is therefore written						き ; ち
203	*Tikai* "near" is written						きち
204	Which is *sa*? (a) き (b) さ (c) ち						ちかい
205	(a) き is ___ ,						(b)
206	and the third, (c) ち , is ___ .						*ki*
207	The H sign for *tu* is つ . Copy and practice.						*ti*

#	Content						Answer
208	*Tuti* "earth" is written						つ *tu* (repeated)
209	あつい is read _____ .						つち
210	*Katuo* "bonito" is written						*atui* ("hot")
211	*Setu* "theory, opinion" is written						かつお
212	*Utu* "to hit" is written—						せつ

213	The sign つ also has a special function: when used before other *kana* for sounds with an initial *k, s, t* or *p* (discussed later), it may double the consonant. For example, *sitta* "knew" is written *si*+*tu*+*ta*, that is, しった. Similarly, *katta* "bought" is written	うつ
214	*kotti* (=*kotira*) "this direction" is written	かった
215	*sotti* (=*sotira*) "that direction" is written	こっち
216	*kakko* "brackets" is written	そっち
217	and *atta* "was" is written	かっこ
218	Sometimes only the context will tell whether つ is to be read as a full syllable *tu*, or used instead to double the following consonant. We saw just above, for example, that あった was the way to write _____ "was,"	あった
219	but つ would have to be read as a full syllable in あつた if it were, for example, the place-name A __ __ *ta* that was meant.	*atta*
220	To distinguish these two uses of つ , most modern writing uses the ordinary size of *kana* sign for the full syllable, and a smaller one written slightly to the right of centre (or slightly lower when writing sideways) to double the following c_____ t.	*Atuta*
221	This practice will be followed from now on in this course, so that あった will represent _____	consonant
222	and あつた _____.	*Atuta*

34

223	The next sign, the one for *te*, is て . Copy and practice the writing of it. て *te* て *te* て *te*	*atta*
224	H *te* is written	て *te* (repeated)
225	きって is read _____.	て
226	(But remember, あ つ さ is read_____.)	*kitte* ("stamp")
227	*Aite* "companion, opponent" is written	*atusa* ("heat")
228	*Tetu* "iron" is written	あいて
229	*Tate* "upright" is written	てつ
230	The sign for *to* is と . Copy and practice. と *to* と *to* と *to*	たて
231	こと is read _____.	' と *to* (etc.)
232	*Toki* "time" is written	*koto* ("matter")
233	*Ito* "thread" is written	とき
234	*Tosi* "year" is written	いと
235	そと is read _____.	とし
236	*Sotto* "softly" is written	*soto* ("outside")
237	Now try a short review of the *kana* you have learned so far. Romanize the following words, and check your readings when you have finished all ten.	そっと

	10.	9.	8.	7.	6.	5.	4.	3.	2.	1.
	く	た	そ	お	あ	せ	お	ち	う	こ
	ち	て	っ	す	つ	き	け	か	つ	え
	と	し	さ		い					て

1. _____ 2. _____ 3. _____ 4. _____ 5. _____

6. _____ 7. _____ 8. _____ 9. _____ 10. _____

238

Now write the following words in H, and check your writing when you have finished all five.

1. *kaki* "oyster" 2. *asi* "foot, leg" 3. *sita* "lower part" 4. *soto* "outside" 5. *kusa* "grass"

1. *koe* ("voice")
2. *utte* ("selling")
3. *tikai* ("near")
4. *oke* ("tub")
5. *seki* ("seat")
6. *atusa* ("heat")
7. *o-susi* ("rice-cake")
8. *sotto* ("softly")
9. *tate* ("upright")
10. *kuti* ("mouth")

If you have mistaken a *kana* sign, write it out until you feel sure you know it or, if you prefer, review the section dealing with that particular *kana*.

1. かき 2. あし 3. した
4. そと 5. くさ

IV. THE BASIC SIGNS: *na* to *mo*

Before going on to the new signs, write and check those you have met already, as you did before.

1. si		2. ki		3. te		4. ti		5. ko	
6. ka		7. u		8. su		9. ta		10. e	
11. sa		12. so		13. i		14. tu		15. ke	
16. a		17. ku		18. to		19. o		20. se	

1. し　2. き　3. て　4. ち　5. こ

6. か　7. う　8. す　9. た　10. え

11. さ　12. そ　13. い　14. つ　15. け

16. あ　17. く　18. と　19. お　20. せ

239	After *t*, the next group of sounds begins with ___.	
240	The first of these sounds is *na*, written な. Copy and practice this: ニ ナ ナ な *na* な *na*	*n*
241	な か is read _____.	ーナナーな *na* (etc.)
242	*Naku* "to cry" is written	*naka* ("inside")
243	*Kana* "*kana* sign" is written	なく
244	Distinguish な *na* from た, which is ____.	かな
245	Thus, た な is read _____,	*ta*
246	and *anata* "you" is written	*tana* ("shelf")
247	*Nai* "to be not" is written	あなた
248	*Nanatu* "seven" is written	ない
249	The next sound is *ni*, written に. Practice this. 丨 に に *ni* に *ni*	ななつ
250	*Nani* "what?" is written	丨 に に *ni* (etc.)
251	に く is read _____.	なに
252	*Tani* "valley" is written	*niku* ("meat")

#		Answer
253	*Kuni* "country" is written	たに
254	*Ani* "elder brother" is written	くに
255	Copy and practice the writing of *nu*. い　ぬ　*nu*　ぬ　*nu*	あに
256	いぬ is read _____.	いぬ *nu*(etc.)
257	*Kinu* "silk" is written	*inu* ("dog")
258	*Ainu*, the name for the aborigines of Japan, is written	きぬ
259	しぬ is read _____.	あいぬ
260	*Nuu* "to sew" is written	*sinu* ("to die")
261	*Nuku* "to extract" is written	ぬう
262	Next learn to write *ne* ね り　ね　*ne*　ね　*ne*	ぬく
263	*Neko* "cat" is written	｜ね *ne*(etc.)
264	*Ane* "elder sister" is written	ねこ
265	かね is read _____.	あね
266	*Ne* "root" is written	*kane* ("money")
267	Which is *ine* "rice plant"? (a) いぬ (b) いね	ね
268	What, then, is the reading of (a) いぬ?	(b)

#		Answer
269	Thus, *nu* is written ___ and *ne* ___	*inu* ("dog")
270	If you confused these two, remember that *ne* has a first stroke which goes straight down like a *ne* "root." Try writing *ne* again.	ぬ ね
271	H *no* has only one stroke: の . Practice this. の *no* の *no* の *no*	ね
272	*No* "of; moor" is written ___	の *no* (repeated)
273	*Kono* "this" is written ___	の
274	*Ano* "that" is written ___	この
275	としうえの is read _____.	あの
276	*Tosisita no* "younger" is written ___	*tosiue no* ("older")
277	*Natu no kusa* "the grass of summer" is written ___	としし たの
278	*Kita no kuni* "a country of the north" is written ___	なつ の くさ
279	*Ha* is written は . Copy and practice. ↓｜ ｜ーは↓ *ha* は *ha*	きたの くに
280	*Haha* "mother" is written ___	｜ ｜ーは *ha* (etc.)
281	*Hai* "yes" is written ___	はは

282	*Ha* "leaf; tooth" is written			はい
283	therefore はな is read _____.			は
284	Thus, な is ___, and は is ___,			*hana* ("flower; nose")
285	and *hana* "flower; nose" is written			*na; ha*
286	Do not worry about confusing these two signs, however, because は is used to write the particle pronounced *wa*, and you will soon come to know it very well. Thus, いぬには is read _____;			はな
287	いねには is read _____;			*inu ni wa* ("on the dog")
288	and *hana no ue ni wa* "on the flower/nose" is written			*ine ni wa* ("on the rice plant")
289	The sign for *hi* is written ひ or, sometimes, in two strokes ひ. Practice this sign.			はなのう えには
290	Thus, *hi* "day; sun; fire" is written			ひ *hi* (etc.)
291	ひくい is read _____.			ひ
292	*Hiniti* "(number of) days" is written			*hikui* ("low")
293	*Hito* "person" is written			ひにち
294	ひとのはなには is read _____.			ひと
295	The sign for *hu* (*fu*) is ふ. Follow the direction of the strokes carefully in practicing the writing.			*hito no hana ni wa* ("on the person's nose")

３	い３	い３ヾ	*hu*	３	い３	い３い	*hu*	い３い	*hu*	

296	Note that, if the pen was not taken from the paper, the sign would look like this: ᘐ . Now practice the sign several times.							３ い３ い３ *hu* (etc.)

	い３い	*hu*	い３い	*hu*						

297	*Hu* "urban prefecture" is written				い３い *hu*(repeated)
298	*Hune* "ship" is written				い３い
299	ふえ is read _____ .				い３ね
300	*Hutatu* "two" is written				*hue* ("flute")
301	い３ く is read _____ .				ふたつ
302	*Suihu* "sailor" is written				*huku* ("clothes")

303	The H sign for *he* is へ , written from left to right. Practice this.						すいふ

へ	*he*	へ	*he*	へ	*he*				

304	*Hei* "wall" is written				へ *he*(repeated)
305	*Heta na* "unskilful" is written				へい
306	へ い た い is read _____				へたな
307	*Heiti* "level ground" is written				*heitai* ("soldier")
308	*Suihei* "horizon" is written				へいち

309	An important use of へ is to write the particle *e* "to(wards)." Thus, おとこはいえへはしっていった is read _____ ;	すいへい
310	and *Sikoku e iku* "to go to Sikoku" is written [ ][ ][ ][ ][ ][ ]	*Otoko wa ie e hasitte itta* ("the man ran to the house")
311	The last initial *h* sound, *ho*, is written ほ. Copy and practice the writing of it. [丨↓][丨ー→][丨ー↓][ほ↓][*ho*][ほ][*ho*] [ ][ ][ ][ ][ ][ ]	しこくへ いく
312	ほし is read _____.	丨 丨ー 丨ーほ *ho* (etc.)
313	*Hone* "bone" is written [ ][ ][ ]	*hosi* ("star")
314	*Hosoi* "slender, fine" is written [ ][ ][ ][✕]	ほね
315	*Ho wa akai* "the sail is red" is written [ ][ ][ ][ ][ ]	ほそい
316	Thus, *ha* (=particle *wa*) is written [ ], and *ho* is written [ ]	ほはあ かい
317	One of the following words contains the sign for *ho*. What is the reading of this word? _____ (a) はたけ　(b) ほとけ	は；ほ
318	What is the reading, then, of (a) はたけ ?	*hotoke* ("Buddha")
319	Now write in H *ho no sita ni wa* "under the sail." [ ][ ][ ][ ][ ][ ]	*hatake* ("[dry] field")
320	After the sounds beginning with *h* come those beginning with ____.	ほのした には

321	The first of these, *ma*, is written ま	
	⇄ 〒→ ↓ま ma ま ma	m

322	Thus, た ま is read _____.	ー ニ ま *ma* (etc.)
323	*Mata* "also, again" is written ☐ ☐ ☐	*tama* ("ball; jewel")
324	ま こ と に is read _____.	また
325	*Ima* "now" is written ☐ ☐ ☐	*makoto ni* ("truly")
326	*Kuma* "bear" is written ☐ ☐ ☐	いま
327	*Matu* "pine tree" is written ☐ ☐ ☐	くま
328	*Sima* "island" is written ☐ ☐ ☐	まつ
329	*Uma* "horse" is written ☐ ☐ ☐	しま
330	Distinguish ま *ma* from は ___ and ほ ___.	うま
331	ほ ね の な ま え は , for example, is read _____.	*ha; ho*
332	Now write for yourself this same phrase *hone no namae wa* "the name of the bone": ☐ ☐ ☐ ☐ ☐ ☐ ☐	*hone no namae wa* ("the name of the bone")
333	If you wrote this correctly, omit this and the next two frames. If you confused は , ほ and ま , remember that は and ほ , the signs for sounds beginning with *h*, are in two *hal* __ __ __, left and right;	ほねの なまえ は
334	and that ま *ma* is very like the shape and sound of £, representing *mo* __ __ y.	halves

335	With this in mind, try writing *hone no namae wa* again.	money
336	The sign for *mi* is み . Practice this.	ほねの なまえ は
	ゑ み ⟨mi⟩ み ⟨mi⟩	
337	Thus, す み is read _____ .	みみ ⟨mi⟩(etc.)
338	*Miti* "road" is written	*sumi* ("inside corner")
339	みなさま is read _____ .	みち
340	*Mita koto no nai koinu* "a puppy I have never seen" is written	*mina-sama* ([respectful] "everyone")
341	かみ is read _____ .	みたことのな いこいぬ
342	*Kami-sama* (respectful) "god" is written	*kami* ("god; paper; hair")
343	*Tatami* "mat flooring" is written	かみさま
344	*Mimi* "ear" is written	たたみ
345	H *mu* is written む . Practice this.	みみ
	⌐も む ⟨mu⟩ む ⟨mu⟩	
346	むし then, is read _____ .	⌐もむ ⟨mu⟩(etc.)
347	*Mukasi* "former times" is written	*musi* ("insect")
348	*Umu* "to give birth to" is written	むかし

349	むっつ is read _____.	うむ
350	*Nomu* "to drink" is written	*muttu* ("six")
351	*Sumu* "to live" is written	のむ
352	The sign for *me* is め. Copy and practice. 〵 め／ *me* め *me*	すむ
353	Thus, あ め is read _____.	〵 め *me*(etc.)
354	*Kome* "(uncooked) rice" is written	*ame* ("rain")
355	*Kosame* "drizzle" is written	こめ
356	*Ume* "plum tree" is written	こさめ
357	Which of these is read *me*? (a) め (b) ぬ	うめ
358	What, then, is (b) ぬ ?	(a)
359	Thus, い ぬ の た め に is read _____;	*nu*
360	and *me no itai mesu-inu* "a bitch with sore eyes" is written	*inu no tame ni* ("for the sake of the dog")
361	If you wrote it correctly, omit this and the next frame. If you confused ぬ *nu* and め *me*, remember that both the sign ぬ *nu* and the object signified by い ぬ *inu* "dog" have t___ ___ls.	め の い た い め す い ぬ
362	Remembering this, write *mesu-inu wa koinu no tame ni sinu* "the bitch dies for the sake of its pup."	tails

No.	Content	Answer
363	The last *m* sound, *mo*, is written も ↓し　そ　↘も　*mo*　も　*mo*	めすいぬは こいぬのた めにしぬ
364	Thus, もの is read _____ .	しても *mo*(etc.)
365	*Kaimono* "shopping" is written	*mono* ("thing")
366	*Amimono* "knitting" is written	かいもの
367	*Tatemono* "building" is written	あみもの
368	しも is read _____ .	たてもの
369	*Momo* "peach" is written	*simo* ("frost")
370	*Setomono* "china" is written	もも
371	Now that you have met nearly three-quarters of the basic H signs, test yourself by transcribing the sentences below into or from *kana*, checking each one as you go. *Ueno e ikimasu ka* "Will you go to Ueno?"	せともの
372	*Itta koto no nai Ise* "Ise, where I have never been"	うえのへい きますか
373	*Anata no mae no koinu* "The puppy in front of you"	いったこと のないいせ
374	*Keisatu to hanasite mo* "Even if you talk to the police"	あなたのま えのこいぬ
375	*Sono heitai wa itu hune ni imasita ka* "When was that soldier on the ship?"	けいさつと はなしても

376	*Kami-no-ke no akai hito* "A person with red hair"	そのへいた いはいつふ ねにいまし たか
377	*Ti mo niku mo nai hone wa* "The bone with neither blood nor meat"	かみ のけの あかい ひと
378	ひ の ため に あつ い う ち	ちもにくも ないほねは
379	あ の あ お い た て も の に す む と お も い ます	*Hi no tame ni atui uti* ("a house hot because of the sun")
380	ち か く の ひ と の い う こ と に つ い て き く	*Ano aoi tatemono ni sumu to omoimasu* ("I think he will live in that blue house")
	If you mistook a *kana* sign once only in the last ten examples, write it out WITH ITS READING (e.g. ま *ma*) until you are sure you know it. If you mistook the same *kana* sign more than once, review the section above in which it was introduced. Then continue with the next section.	*Tikaku no hito no yuu koto ni tuite kiku* ("to ask about what the local people say")

V. THE BASIC SIGNS: *ya* to *n*

Make sure you remember the signs already met by completing the lines below, and then continue as usual.

1. *tu*		2. *so*		3. *ma*		4. *ka*		5. *to*	
6. *ko*		7. *a*		8. *se*		9. *mi*		10. *hi*	
11. *te*		12. *ho*		13. *ki*		14. *ti*		15. *si*	
16. *su*		17. *ha*		18. *me*		19. *no*		20. *mo*	
21. *i*		22. *ku*		23. *ta*		24. *ni*		25. *hu*	
26. *na*		27. *he*		28. *o*		29. *u*		30. *ne*	
31. *ke*		32. *e*		33. *mu*		34. *nu*		35. *sa*	

1. つ		2. そ		3. ま		4. か		5. と
6. こ		7. あ		8. せ		9. み		10. ひ
11. て		12. ほ		13. き		14. ち		15. し
16. す		17. は		18. め		19. の		20. も
21. い		22. く		23. た		24. に		25. ふ
26. な		27. へ		28. お		29. う		30. ね
31. け		32. え		33. む		34. ぬ		35. さ

381	Having dealt with initial *m* sounds, the next are those beginning with _____.	
382	There are only three of these, *ya*, *yu* and *yo*. *Ya* is written や . Practice in the usual way. う ら や *ya* や *ya*	*y*
383	Thus, *ya* "arrow" is written	う ら や *ya* (etc.)
384	やま is read _____.	や
385	*Yamato*, a place-name once used for Japan as a whole, is written	*yama* ("mountain")
386	*Yaoya* "greengrocer" is written	やまと
387	はやく is read _____.	やおや
388	*Yaseta* "thin" is written	*hayaku* ("quickly, early")
389	*Komeya* "rice merchant" is written	やせた
390	へや is read _____.	こめや
391	Since there is no *i* sound preceded by *y*, the next sound is *y*__.	*heya* ("room")
392	The sign for *yu* is ゆ . Practice this. ゆ ゆ *yu* ゆ *yu*	*yu*

393	Thus, お ゆ is read _____.	いゆ *yu* (etc.)
394	*Yumi* "bow (weapon)" is written	*o-yu* ("hot water")
395	ゆ め is read _____.	ゆ み
396	*Yuka* "floor" is written	*yume* ("dream")
397	ゆ き is read _____.	ゆ か
398	つ ゆ is read _____.	*yuki* ("snow")
399	Remember that ゆ is NOT used in writing *yuu* "to say," the *kana* for this being	*tuyu* ("dew")
400	There being no *e* preceded by *y*, the only other initial *y* sound is _____.	いう
401	*Yo* is written よ . Practice writing this, taking care not to let the second, vertical stroke cut the horizontal. よ *yo* よ *yo*	*yo*
402	Hence, よ く is read _____.	゛よ *yo* (etc.)
403	*Yoku yomu* "to read well" is written	*yoku* ("well")
404	*Mi yo* (brusque) "Look!" is written	よくよむ
405	*Yo-no-naka* "the world, society" is written	みよ
406	よみやすい is read_____.	よのなか
407	There is a complete set of five sounds beginning with *r*, however, namely *ra*, _____, _____, _____, _____.	*yomi-yasui* ("easy to read")

408	*Ra* is written ら . Copy and practice.								*ri, ru, re, ro*
	ら	ら	*ra*	ら	*ra*				
409	むら is therefore read _____.								ら *ra* (etc.)
410	The place-name *Urasima* is written								*mura* ("village")
411	*Tumaranai* "trivial, worthless" is written								うらしま
412	てら is read _____.								つまらない
413	*Ri* is written り . Practice this.								*tera* ("Buddhist temple")
	り	り	*ri*	り	*ri*				
414	あります is read _____.								り *ri* (etc.)
415	*Ari* "ant" is written								*arimasu* ("exists")
416	ゆり is read _____.								あり
417	*Muri* "unreasonableness" is written				✕				*yuri* ("lily")
418	*Riku* "land" is written								むり
419	The sign for *ru* is る . Copy and practice.								りく
	る	る	*ru*	る	*ru*	る	*ru*		
420	ある then, is read _____.								る *ru* (repeated)

421	こしかける is read _____.			aru ("to exist")
422	*Miru* "to see" is written			kosikakeru ("to sit down")
423	*Nurui* "tepid" is written			みる
424	るす is read _____.			ぬるい
425	*Re* is written れ . Learn the writing of this. ↓| れ *re* れ *re* □□□□□□□□			rusu ("absence [from home]")
426	Thus, *sore* "that (one)" is written ▦			lれ *re* (etc.)
427	きれいな is read _____.			それ
428	*Are* "that (one over there)" is written ▦			kirei na ("pretty")
429	しつれい is read _____.			あれ
430	Do not confuse れ *re* with ね ___.			siturei ("rudeness")
431	Distinguish ね *ne* by remembering that, just as *nu* and *ne* have the same consonant, so ぬ and □ have the same tail.			ne
432	The last sound beginning with *r* is *ro*, written ろ . Practice writing this as before until you are satisfied. ろ *ro* ろ *ro* □□□□□□□			ね
433	Thus, いろ is read _____.			ろ *ro* (repeated)
434	*Iroiro na* "various, all kinds of" is written □□□□□□			iro ("colour")
435	しろ is read _____.			いろいろな
436	What, then, is しる ?			siro ("castle")

437	Thus, る is ____, and ろ is ____.	*siru* ("to know")
438	ひろめる is read _____ ;	*ru*; *ro*
439	and *huro ni iru* "to be in the bath" is written □ □ □ □ □	*hiromeru* ("to widen, to spread")
440	The first sound with an initial *w* is *wa*, written わ. Write this until you feel you know it. ↓| わ *wa* わ *wa* □ □ □ □ □ □ □ □ □ □ □ □ □	ふろに いる
441	The sound *wa* is always written with this sign unless it is the particle *wa*, when it is written ⌐□	1 わ *wa* (etc.)
442	*Wa* "wheel" is therefore written ⌐□	は
443	*wa wa* "(as for) the wheel," consisting of noun and particle, is written □□	わ
444	and, similarly, *hanawa wa* "(as for) the wreath" is written □□□	わは
445	わたしたち then, is read _____,	はなわは
446	and *saiwai ni* "fortunately" is written □□□□	*watasitati* ("we")
447	Identify the following three *kana*: (a) れ ____ (b) わ ____ (c) ね ____	さいわ いに
448	If you mistook any of these, write it out WITH ITS READING until you know it beyond doubt, remembering that *wa* is rounded like a *wa* ("wheel"). When you have done this, or if you made no mistake, continue by transcribing the following. わ か れ _____ .	(a) *re* (b) *wa* (c) *ne*
449	*Wasureru* "to forget" □ □ □ □ ⊠	*wakare* ("parting")

450	and これはわすれたふ ねにありましたね _____.	わすれる
451	There being no *u* sound preceded by *w*, the next two sounds are *wi* and _____.	*Kore wa wasureta hune ni arimasita ne* ("This was in the forgotten ship, wasn't it")
452	Since both have lost their initial consonant in standard speech, let us show this by writing them (*w*)*i* and _____.	*we*
453	H (*w*)*i* is written ゐ . Practice this and distinguish it in your mind from る , which is _____.	(*w*)*e*
454	ゐ (*w*)*i* ゐ (*w*)*i*	*ru*
455	When the consonant sound in (*w*)*i* disappeared, it left the vowel __ alone.	ゐ (*w*)*i* (repeated)
456	But since there was already a *kana* sign for *i*, the one for (*w*)*i* became un _____ry.	*i*
457	The modern simplified system of writing therefore ignores the sign ゐ , and uses instead [ ] , the one for the simple vowel *i*.	unnecessary
458	Thus *iru* "to be," formerly written ゐ る , is now written [ ] る .	い
459	and *kurai* "degree, extent," formerly written くら[ ] , is now written くら[ ]	い
460	(W)*e* has similarly been replaced, for the same reasons, by __.	ゐ;い

461	Practice the writing of *(w)e* 急 so that you will immediately recognize it, for you will eventually meet it in your study of Japanese. 急 急 | *(w)e* | 急 | *(w)e* | | | | | | |	*e*
462	*Koe* "voice," then, which used to be written こ 急 in H, is now written ☐☐	急急 *(w)e* (etc.)
463	and *e* "picture," which used to be written 急 in H, is now written ☐	こ え
464	The last basic H sign representing a consonant and vowel is *wo*, written を . Practice this until you can not only recognize it but write it without fail yourself, for it is a very common sign. を を | *wo* | を | *wo* | | | | | | |	え
465	Since the initial consonant sound disappeared in *wo* as it did in *(w)i* and *(w)e*, we can indicate this in the same way by writing it _____.	一 を を *(w)o* (etc.)
466	In all cases but one, *(w)o* too is similarly replaced in *kana* by the sign for the vowel alone, in this case ___, written ☐	*(w)o*
467	Thus, *sao* "pole," which used to be written さ を in H, is now written ☐☐	*o;* お
468	and *otoko* "man" which used to be written をとこ in H, is now written ☐☐☐	さ お
469	But, unlike ゐ and 急 , を *(w)o* still keeps one important role: it is the sign used for the accusative particle ___.	おとこ

56

470	Hence, か み を か う is read _____ ;	o
471	and *kosi o kakeru* "to sit down" is written	*kami o kau* ("to buy paper")
472	There is just one other basic sign, that used for an *n* at the end of a syllable (e.g. *hoN*, *zaNneN*). This is written ん and should be practiced. ん *n* ん *n* ん *n*	こしを かける
473	Thus, ほん is read _____ .	ん *n* (repeated)
474	へんな is read _____ .	*hon* ("book")
475	*Itinen* "one year" is written	*hen na* ("strange")
476	*Nannen* "what year, how many years" is written	いち ねん
477	*Nihon* "Japan" is written	なん ねん
478	and あんま is read _____ .	にほん
479	Now that you have covered all the basic H signs, just check your memory of them by transcribing the following sentences into *kana* as carefully as possible. Correct your transcription where necessary after each sentence. *Takusan no o-yu o wakasite kuremasita.* "He (kindly) boiled a lot of hot water."	*anma* ("massage." Note that such words are sometimes romanized with a double *m* as *amma* etc.; in this case ん can be said to double the following *m*)

480

Itu o-huro ni hairimasita ka. "When did you have a bath?"

たくさんの
おゆをわか
してくれま
した

481

Sore wa inu koya no naka ni arimasen yo.
"It isn't in the dog kennel!"

いつおふろ
にはいりま
したか

482

Are wa sora o watatte iku tori ka mo siremasen.
"That may be a bird going across the sky"

それはいぬ
こやのなか
にありませ
んよ

483

Watasi no mita kirei na heya wa ano ie ni arimasu.
"The pretty room I saw is in that house."

あれはそら
をわたって
いくとりか
もしれませ
ん

If you made only one mistake with any particular *kana*, relearn it to your satisfaction.

If you repeated a mistake over the same *kana* sign, review the section of the course in which it was introduced.

わたしのみ
たきれいな
へやはあの
いえにあり
ます

VI. VOICED SOUNDS

Having learned all the basic H signs, you now have only to see how some of them can be modified to produce related sounds or read together as compound sounds. None of these points will cause you any difficulty.

The modified sounds, for example, are "thickened" or voiced ones shown merely by adding two small strokes ＼ (called *nigori* or *dakuten* in Japanese) or a small circle ○ to certain of the signs you have already learned.

H ga—go

484	Thus か, read *ka*, gives が, read *ga*. Similarly: き *ki* gives [ ] *gi*;	
485	く *ku* gives *gu*;	ぎ
486	け *ke* gives *ge*; and	ぐ
487	こ *ko* gives *go*.	げ
488	Hence, が is used for the particle ＿＿＿,	ご
489	and *gaikoku* "foreign country" is written [ ][ ][ ][ ]	*ga*
490	Similarly, ぎ ん is read ＿＿＿＿＿,	がいこく
491	and *mugi* "barley, wheat" is written [ ][ ][✗]	*gin* ("silver")
492	ぐ ん is read ＿＿＿＿,	むぎ
493	and *gunkan* "warship" is written [ ][ ][ ][ ]	*gun* ("rural district")
494	げ い is read ＿＿＿＿,	ぐんかん
495	and *ageru* "to raise" is written [ ][ ][✗]	*gei* ("artistic skill")
496	ご ご is read ＿＿＿＿＿,	あげる
497	and *gohan* "rice, a meal" is written [ ][ ][ ]	*gogo* ("afternoon")

498	Now that you have seen how the addition of the two *nigori* strokes 〟 to the signs for *ka*, *ki*, *ku*, *ke* and *ko* gives the signs for the voiced sounds *ga*, _____, _____, _____, and _____,	ごはん
499	transcribe the following words into either *kana* or roman script, as appropriate. *gakusei* "student" [ ][ ][ ][ ]	*gi, gu, ge; go*
500	ぎむ _____;	がくせい
501	ぐあい _____;	*gimu* ("duty")
502	*genki na* "vigorous" [ ][ ][ ][ ]	*guai* ("condition, state")
503	ごがつ _____;	げんきな
504	*sageru* "to lower" [ ][ ][ ]	*gogatu* ("May")
505	*kagu* "to smell" [ ][ ]	さげる
506	こちらがわ_____;	かぐ
507	*gomen* "pardon" [ ][ ][ ]	*kotiragawa* ("this side")
508	ふしぎに _____;	ごめん
509	なにがありますか _____	*husigi ni* ("strangely")
510	Just as か *ka* etc. give が *ga* etc., so さ *sa* gives ざ *za*; し *si* (*shi*) gives [ ] *zi* (*ji*);	*nani ga arimasu ka* ("what is there?")
511	す *su* gives [ ] *zu*;	じ
512	せ *se* gives [ ];	ず
513	and そ *so* gives [ ].	ぜ *ze*

514	Transcribe, then, the following: ぎんざ _____ .	ぞ *zo*
515	かんじ _____ ;	*Ginza* (place-name)
516	ちず _____ ;	*kanzi* ("feeling; Chinese character")
517	ぜんぜん _____ ;	*tizu* ("map")
518	ぞんじる _____ ;	*zenzen* ("completely")
519	*mizu* "(cold) water"	*zonziru* ([humble] "to think")
520	*zeikin* "tax"	み ず
521	*zutto* "throughout, far more"	ぜいきん
522	*zannen na* "regrettable"	ずっと
523	た *ta* etc. similarly become だ *da* etc. Thus, だった is read _____ ;	ざんね んな
524	でした is read _____ ;	*datta* ("was")
525	and どこ is read _____ .	*desita* ("was")
526	ぢ and づ , however, are romanized as *zi* and *zu* respectively, since the sounds they represent are the same as those for じ ___ and □ _____ .	*doko* ("where?")
527	ぢ and づ are little used now, because their sounds *zi* and *zu* can already be written with the signs and □	*zi* ; ず *zu*
528	They are in fact used only in two cases: (i) when they immediately follow ち or つ respectively in the same word, e.g. *tizimeru* "to shrink" is written ち □ め る	じ ; ず
529	and *tuzuku* "to continue" is written つ □ く	ぢ
530	(ii) when *ti* and *tu* become voiced (i.e., become *zi* and *zu* respectively) as a result of becoming part of a compound word.	づ

#		
	Thus, *hana* "nose" + *ti* "blood" = *hanazi* "nosebleed," written [ ][ ][ ]	
531	and *mika* (for *mikka* "three days") + *tuki* "moon" = *mika-zuki* "three-day moon, crescent moon," written [ ][ ][ ]	はなぢ
532	Remembering these two kinds of exceptional spelling, transcribe the following words containing the voiced syllables *da, zi, zu,* etc. でんき ——————;	みかづき
533	にさんど ——————————;	denki ("electricity")
534	*desu* "is"	nisando ("two or three times")
535	*tuzuku* "to continue" [ ][ ][ ]	です
536	だんだん ——————;	つづく
537	*zisin* "earthquake" [ ][ ]	dandan ("gradually")
538	どれ ——;	じしん
539	*denwa* "telephone" [ ][ ][ ]	dore ("which?")
540	The last consonant to become fully voiced, *h*, changes straightforwardly to *b* with all vowels. That is, は *ha*, ひ *hi*, ふ *hu*, へ *he* and ほ *ho* become [ ] *ba*, [ ] ——, [ ] ——, ——, and ——, respectively.	でんわ
541	Thus, ばんごはん is ——————.	ば び *bi*, ぶ *bu*, べ *be*; ぼ *bo*
542	*zabuton* "cushion" is [ ][ ][ ][ ]	ban-gohan ("evening meal")
543	べいこくじん is ——————;	ざぶとん
544	*boku* (familiar) "I" is [ ][ ]	Beikokuzin ("American")

545	*oba* "aunt" is							ぼく
546	*tabi* "journey; Japanese sock" is							おば
547	*benri na* "convenient" is				⊠			たび
548	ぼんやりと is _____;							べんりな
549	びっくりする is _____;							*bonyari to* ("vaguely")
550	and *bubun* "part" is							*bikkuri suru* ("to be surprised")
551	The signs は , ひ etc. for *ha, hi* etc. also take the semi-voicing sign ○ (*handaku*) to represent the initial sound *p*. Thus, ぱ represents *pa*, ☐ *pi*, ☐ ___, ☐ ___, and ☐ ___.							ぶぶん
552	Hence, へんぴな is _____;							ぴ ぷ *pu;* ぺ *pe;* ぽ *po*
553	にんぷ is _____;							*henpi na* ("remote")
554	ぺらぺら is _____;							*ninpu* ("labourer")
555	しんぽ is _____;							*perapera* ("fluently")
556	*sinpai* "anxiety" is							*sinpo* ("progress")
557	*sanpo* "walk" is							しんぱい
558	and *enpitu* "pencil" is							さんぽ
559	Like *k, t* and *s*, a *p* can be doubled by a preceding つ , now usually written smaller and slightly off centre in this use. For example, りっぱ な is _____;							えんぴ つ
560	and *kippu* "ticket" is							*rippa na* ("splendid")
								きっぷ

VII. COMBINED SOUNDS AND MISCELLANEOUS SIGNS

Except for the sign ⊃ used to double a following consonant, all the *kana* we have met so far represented simple, single sounds.   But Japanese also contains compound sounds and, when these are written in *kana*, it is necessary to read two or more *kana* signs together.

Long vowels are a case in point, although, in the modern *kana* spelling, the only one with unexpected features in its written form is the long vowel *oo*.

561	We have already met *tiisai* "small," written 	
562	and long *a*, *u* and *e* vowels are likewise written quite regularly in *kana* by adding a sign for a single v___ ___ ___l, as in the romanization.	ちいさ い
563	Thus, *kuuki* "atmosphere" is written	vowel
564	*o-kaasan* (respectful) "mother" is written 	くうき
565	and *o-neesan* (respectful) "elder sister" is written 	おかあ さん
566	A long *o* sound, however, is only written in *kana* by adding お when this replaces a ほ sign in the old *kana* spelling. For example, *ooi* "numerous," which used to be written おほい, is now written お〼い	おねえ さん
567	There is no way of telling from the word itself whether it is of this type, but there are only a few important words written in this way. They are: (i) *ooi* "numerous"	お
568	(ii) *ookii* "big"	おおい

No.	Content	Answer
569	and *oo-* "big" as a prefix, e.g., *oo-warai* "hearty laughter"	おおき い
570	*oo-hasi* "large bridge"	おおわらい
571	(iii) *tooru* "to go through/along"	おおはし
572	and related words such as *toosu* "to send through/along"	とおる
573	*toori* "street, way"	とおす
574	and *oo-doori* "main street"　お　　ど　　り	とおり
575	(iv) *koori* "ice"	おおどおり
576	Usually, however, long *o* is written in *kana* as *o+u*, i.e. as	こおり
577	Words written this way include *hikooki* "airplane"	おう
578	*oosama* "king"	ひこうき
579	and *boosi* "hat"	おうさま
580	Conversely, remember in reading *kana* that う *u* following a sound ending in *o* may be there to l_____then the *o*,	ぼうし
581	or to be read as a se_____te sound.	lengthen
582	Only the context will tell you whether it is part of a long vowel: うんどう	separate
583	そうだん _____,	*undoo*("exercise")
584	or whether it is to be kept separate: だんのうら _____,	*soodan*("consultation")
585	はのうえに _____;	*Dannoura* (place-name)

586	But with practice, and as you come to know more Japanese words, the choice will not be difficult. The same is true of the reading of *kana* for diphthongs such as *tya* (*cha*), *syu* (*shu*), *byo*, etc. *Tya* (*cha*) is written as *ti* + *ya*, i.e. ち や similarly *syu* (*shu*) is *si* + *yu*, i.e. ☐☐	*ha no ue ni* ("on the leaf/tooth")
587	and *byo* is written ____ + ____ , i.e. ☐☒	し ゆ
588	Thus, such compound sounds are written with a sign for a sound ending in __, plus one for the appropriate sound beginning with __.	*bi* + *yo*; びょ
589	The context will again tell you whether these signs represent separate or compound sounds. ひや , for example, would be kept separate in おひや _____ , a polite word for "water";	*i*; *y*
590	but read together in ひやく _____ meaning "100."	*o-hiya*
591	Often, however, the reading is helped by using a smaller や etc. written slightly off centre when it is part of a compound sound, like つ when it is used to d_____le a consonant.	*hyaku*
592	*Hyaku* "100," then will often be written ひ☐☐ or ひ☐☐	double
593	and *o-tya* "tea" often written ☐☐☐	ひ や or ひ や く
594	Such compound sounds can, of course, have long vowels. These are written in the same way as ordinary long vowels; that is, they take an extra single vowel except in the case of long *o*, when __ is added instead.	おちゃ

#		
595	For example, *tyuu* (*chuu*) is written *ti* + *yu* + *u*, in *kana* □ □ □	*u*
596	and *syuu* (*shuu*) is written __ __ + __ __ + __, in *kana* □ □	ちゅう
597	but *syoo* (*shoo*) is written *si* + *yo* + __.	*si* + *yu* + *u*; しゅう
598	in *kana* □ □ □	*u*
599	and *byoo* is written in *kana* □ □ □ □	しょう
600	Thus, *issyoo kenmei ni* "with all one's might" would be written in H as □ □ □ □ □ □ □ □ □	びょう
601	When the same sound is repeated, it is usual now to repeat the *kana*. Thus, *titi* "father" is normally written □ □	いっしょう けんめい に
602	and *tabitabi* "often" □ □ □ □ □	ち ち
603	There are special repetition signs, however, and occasionally they are still used. If only one *kana* is to be repeated, the sign is 〻 , occupying one writing space. For example, *titi* "father" could be written ち〻 or, in vertical writing, ち	たびた び
604	and *haha* "mother" could be written □ □	〻

605	If TWO OR MORE *kana* are to be repeated, the sign which can be used (in vertical writing only) is 〱 , occupying ALWAYS TWO writing spaces. For example, *itu mo itu mo* "all the time" can be written [いつも〱] and *tabitabi* "often" [たび〱]	はゝ
606	Both ゝ and 〱 can be used with the voicing sign ゛ when needed. Thus, *tada* "only" can be written [たゞ] , and *tokorodokoro* "here and there" [ところ゛]	たび〱 いつも〱
607	Finally, there are a few simple punctuation marks used in modern Japanese writing: 。 for a full stop; 、 for a comma; 「 ┘ or 「……」 for quotation marks. Thus, ちちは、「すぐいく」といった。 or ちちは、「すぐいく」といった。 can be transcribed as *Titi* _____ _____.	たゞ；ところ゛〱
	Now that you have met all the signs you need to read H, transcribe the sentences on the following page to make sure that you remember them all. When you have finished all ten sentences, check your versions with those given at the bottom of the page.	*Titi wa,* "*sugu iku*" *to itta.* ("The father said, 'I will go immediately.' ")

HIRAGANA TEST SENTENCES

6. *Sono huku wa itu kimasu ka.*

   "When do you wear that suit?"

7. *Nitiyoobi ni kimasu.*

   "I wear it on Sundays."

8. *Sono hanasi wa dare mo mina kiite imasu.*

   "Everyone has heard that story."

9. *Itu mo onazi koto o kikimasu nee.*

   "We always hear the same things, don't we?"

10. *Ano hito·wa Nihongo no hon o yonde imasu.*

    "That man is reading a Japanese book."

5. これはめずらしいとおもいます。

4. いまでは「ゐる」を「いる」と、「こゑ」を「こえ」とかきます。

3. あにはがっこうのせんせいです。

2. あのひとのはなはおおきいですね

1. そのぼうしはいくらですか。

1. _____
2. _____
3. _____
4. _____
5. _____

·········· ANSWERS ··········

1. *Sono boosi wa ikura desu ka.*

   ("How much is that hat?")

2. *Ano hito no hana wa ookii desu ne.*

   ("His nose is big, isn't it?")

3. *Ani wa gakkoo no sensei desu.*

   ("My elder brother is a school teacher")

4. *Ima de wa "(w)iru" o "iru" to, "ko(w)e" o "koe*

   to kakimasu.

   ("Nowadays one writes '(w)iru' as 'iru' and

   'ko(w)e' as 'koe.' ")

5. *Kore wa mezurasii to omoimasu.*

   ("I think this is rare.")

·········· ANSWERS ··········

10. あのひとはにほんごのほんをよんでいます。

9. いつもおなじことをききますねえ。

8. そのはなしはだれもみなきいています。

7. にちようびにきます。

6. そのふくはいつきますか。

B. KATAKANA

Almost everything that has been said about H applies to the writing of K: consonants can be doubled by the use of a *tu* sign; voiced consonants are shown by ＼ or ＿ ; diphthongs are formed by the addition of the signs for *ya, yu,* or *yo*; the same punctuation signs are used; the same repetition signs are available in theory, although they are rarely used now in practice; and long vowels are written in the same way, except in foreign words.

There are only two signs peculiar to K, and these appear only in the writing of foreign words: a short line occupying one writing space (│ , or ─ when writing horizontally) lengthens a vowel in foreign words; and a solid dot ● is used to separate words, etc. in foreign phrases. Both these signs are shown with reminders in the examples below.

You were told at the beginning of the course that K is used to the exclusion of H in the writing of proclamations, orders, telegrams, etc.; and that it is used with H in ordinary writing to transcribe special words, mainly those of Western origin. It follows from this that these other words will *always* be written in K. To distinguish them from other words which may *sometimes* be in K according to the type of writing, the examples of them below have been marked with an asterisk, thus: *kokoa* "cocoa."

VIII. THE BASIC SIGNS *a* to *ko*

K a

608	*Katakana* (K) *a* is written ア ア is K __.	
609	Practice the writing of this sign: ⇗ ｱ *a* ⁊ ア *a* ア *a*	*a*

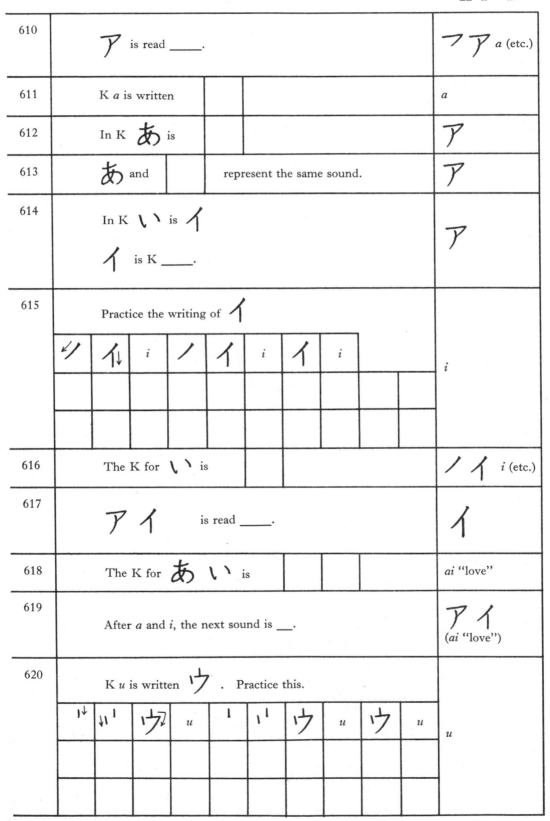

No.	Content	Answer
610	ア is read ____.	フ ア *a* (etc.)
611	K *a* is written	*a*
612	In K あ is	ア
613	あ and represent the same sound.	ア
614	In K い is イ イ is K ____.	ア
615	Practice the writing of イ	*i*
616	The K for い is	ノ イ *i* (etc.)
617	ア イ is read ____.	イ
618	The K for あ い is	*ai* "love"
619	After *a* and *i*, the next sound is __.	ア イ (*ai* "love")
620	K *u* is written ウ . Practice this.	*u*

621	The K for う is ☐	' ' ウ *u* (etc.)
622	If ウ is read __,	ウ (*u*)
623	then アウ is read ____.	*u*
624	The K for *au* "to meet" is ☐☐	*au* ("to meet")
625	イ ウ can be read *iu*; but, as you have seen, when this combination is the verb "to say" it is usually romanized as _ _ _.	アウ
626	The next sound, *e*, is written エ in K. Practice this. → | 丁 | エ | *e* | 一 | 丁 | エ | *e* | エ | *e*	*yuu*
627	The K for え is ☐	一 丁 エ *e* (etc.)
628	Are these signs used for the particle *e* "to(wards)"?	エ
629	The K for うえ is ☐☐	No
630	and that for いえ is ☐☐	ウエ (*ue* "top")
631	We have now met the first four of the five vowel signs, written ☐☐☐☐	イエ (*ie* "house")
632	The remaining one is that for *o*. This is written オ. Copy and practice this. → | 十 | オ | *o* | 一 | 十 | オ | *o* | オ | *o*	アイウエ

633	The K for お is			一十才 o(etc.)
634	If the K for あ is	, and that for い is		才
635	アオイ is read _____.			ア；イ
636	Since the K for う is			aoi ("green, blue")
637	オウ is read _____.			ウ
638	The K for あおい is		☒	ou ("to pursue")
639	and that for おう is			アオイ (aoi "green, blue")
640	お and 才 represent the same sound. Are these signs used to write the particle o?			オウ (ou "to pursue")
641	Since the first initial consonant of the syllabary is ____,			No
642	the next five sounds are ____, ____, ____, ____, ____.			k

643. The K for か is 力. Copy and practice.

ヲ↙カ	ka	フ カ	ka	力	ka	ka, ki, ku, ke, ko

644	ガイガー is read *_____.	フカ ka (etc.)
645	エーカー is read *_____,	*Gaigaa ("Geiger"; — doubles a vowel in foreign words; * shows a word always written in K)
646	オカ is read _____.	*eekaa ("acre")
647	The K for かお is	oka ("hill, mound")

671	and キ コ ウ is read _____.	*kokoa ("cocoa")
672	Having now met the first ten *katakana* signs, transcribe the following five words into roman letters and then check your answers. 5._____ 4.*_____ 3.*_____ 2.*_____ 1._____ コ　　クエカー　　ウエーキ　　ガイガー　　アオイ ケ	*kikou*=*kikoo* ("climate"; remember that, except for foreign words, long vowels are written as in H [see Frames 561–585])
673	Now transcribe the following five words into K and then check your answers. Think particularly about the writing of the long vowels. 1. *kokoa* "cocoa"　2. *kikoo* "climate"　3. *guai* "condition"　4. *yuu* "to say"　5. *keeki* "cake" ⬚⬚ ⬚⬚ ⬚⬚ ⬚⬚ ⬚⬚	1. *aoi* ("green, blue") 2. *Gaigaa* ("Geiger") 3. *Ueeki* ("Wake") 4. *Kueekaa* ("Quaker") 5. *koke* ("moss")
	If you have made any mistakes, write out the *kana* in question until you are sure you can read and write all ten of them correctly.	1.　2.　3. コ　キ　グ コ　コ　ア ア　ウ　イ 4.　5. イ　ケ ウ　ー 　　キ

First, give the K for the following H signs and relearn any you have forgotten.

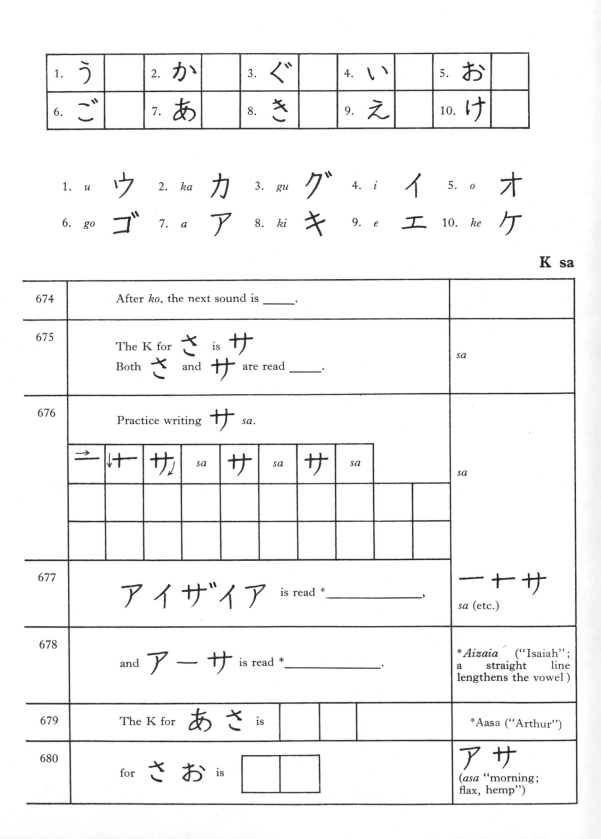

| 1. う | | 2. か | | 3. ぐ | | 4. い | | 5. お | |
| 6. ご | | 7. あ | | 8. き | | 9. え | | 10. け | |

1. *u* ウ   2. *ka* カ   3. *gu* グ   4. *i* イ   5. *o* オ
6. *go* ゴ   7. *a* ア   8. *ki* キ   9. *e* エ   10. *ke* ケ

K sa

674	After *ko*, the next sound is _____.	
675	The K for さ is サ Both さ and サ are read _____.	*sa*
676	Practice writing サ *sa*. → ↓サ サ サ *sa* サ *sa* サ *sa*	*sa*
677	アイザイア is read *_____,	一 十 サ *sa* (etc.)
678	and アーサ is read *_____.	*Aizaia* ("Isaiah"; a straight line lengthens the vowel)
679	The K for あさ is	*Aasa* ("Arthur")
680	for さお is	ア サ (*asa* "morning; flax, hemp")

| 681 | for さき is | | | | サオ
(*sao* "pole") |
| 682 | and for さけ is | | | | サキ
(*saki* "pointed end; tip") |

| 683 | The next sound, *si* (*shi*), is written シ in K. Practice this. | | | | |

| | | ミ | シ | *si* | シ | *si* | シ | *si* | | サケ
(*sake* "rice wine") |

684	Thus, シカゴ is read *_____;	` ` ` ミ ` シ *si* (etc.)
685	コーシカ is read *_____;	*Sikago* ("Chicago")
686	and, since the addition of ＼ (*nigori*) makes シ *si* into ジ —,	*Koosika* ("Corsica")
687	アジ is read *_____.	*zi*
688	The K for こし is			*azi* (=*aziteesyon* "agitation")
689	for かし is			コシ (*kosi* "waist")
690	for しか is			カシ . (*kasi* "cake")
691	and for しお is			シカ (*sika* "deer")
692	K *su* is written ス . Copy and practice this.				

| | ス | ス | *su* | ス | *su* | ス | *su* | | | シオ
(*sio* "salt") |

693	スエズ is read *_____;	フス *su* (etc.)
694	and スキー is read *_____.	*Suezu* ("Suez")
695	*Ekisu* "extract, essence" is written ☐☐☐☐⊠	*sukii* ("ski")
696	and *esu-oo-esu* "SOS" is written ☐☐☐☐☐☐☐☐	エキス
697	アース is read *_____;	エス・オー・エス (a solid dot separates words etc. in foreign phrases)
698	*saakasu* "circus" is written ☐☐☐⊠	*aasu* ("electrical earth")
699	*koosu* "course" is written ☐☐☐	サーカス
700	*gasu* "gas" is written ☐☐	コース
701	and in K おすし is written ☐☐☐⊠	ガス
702	*Su* ス is followed by *se*, written セ Practice this. ↱セ *se* セ *se* セ *se* ☐☐ ☐☐☐☐☐☐☐ ☐☐☐☐☐☐☐	オスシ (*o-susi* "savoury rice-cake")
703	Do not confuse セ, K *se*, with せ, which is the sign for what sound?	つセ

704	Thus, *se* is written		in H, and		in K.	H *se*
705	ガーゼ is read * _____					せ セ
706	and セキ is read _____ .					*gaaze* ("gauze")
707	The K for あ せ is					*seki* ("seat")
708	and for く せ is					ア セ (*ase* "sweat")
709	K *so* is written ソ . Copy the following carefully, noting that the second stroke is written DOWNWARDS. ソ | ソ *so* | ソ *so* | ソ *so*					ク セ (*kuse* "habit")
710	ソ コ is read _____ ;					ヽ ソ *so* (etc.)
711	and ソーセージ is read * _____ .					*soko* ("there")
712	*Soosu* "sauce" is written					* *sooseeji* ("sausage")
713	and *asoko* "(over) there" is written					ソ ー ス
714	The sound which follows *so* is ___ .					ア ソ コ
715	K *ta* is written タ . タ is the K for ___ .					*ta*

716	Practice the writing of タ *ta*.	*ta*

ノ　ク　タ　*ta*　タ　*ta*　タ　*ta*

717	タクシー is read *＿＿＿＿＿＿＿＿ ;	ノ ク タ *ta* (etc.)
718	and *ekusutasii* "ecstasy" is written	*takusii* ("taxi")
719	タイ is read *＿＿＿＿ ;	エクス タシー
720	セーター is read *＿＿＿＿＿＿ ;	*Tai*("Thailand")
721	*gitaa* "guitar" is written	*seetaa* ("sweater")
722	*sooda* "soda" is written	ギター
723	and in K いたい is ☒	ソーダ
724	K *ti* (*chi*) is written チ. Copy and practice.	イタイ (*itai* "painful")

ノ　二　チ　*ti*　チ　*ti*　チ　*ti*

725	The K for ちち is [ ][ ]	´ ニ チ ti (etc.)
726	チーク is read *_____ ;	チ チ (titi "father")
727	and ア ー チ is read *_____.	*tiiku ("teak")
728	*Tiizu "cheese" is written [ ][ ][ ]	*aati ("arch")
729	and in K かち is [ ][ ]	チーズ
730	and ちいさい is [ ][ ][ ][ ]	カ チ (kati "victory; value")
731	The K sign for tu (tsu) is ツ . Practice this carefully. 	い↓	いい↓	ツ	tu	ツ	tu	ツ	tu
									チイサ イ (tiisai "small")
732	The K for つち is [ ][ ]	ヽ ヽヽ ツ tu (etc.)
733	for せつ is [ ][ ]	ツ チ (tuti "earth")
734	for あつい is [ ][ ]	セ ツ (setu "theory, opinion")
735	and for うつ is [ ][ ]	ア ツ イ (atui "hot")
736	Be careful to distinguish ツ tu from シ — in both reading and writing.	ウ ツ (utu "to hit")

737	In シ *si* the third stroke is straight and written upwards (and sometimes hooked like a tick); and the whole sign is written from top to _____.	*si*
738	In ツ *tu*, conversely, the third stroke is rounded and written downwards; and the whole sign is written from l_____ to _____.	bottom
739	K *si*, then, is written	left to right
740	and *tu* is written	シ
741	Thus, シ ツ コ イ is read _____,	ツ
742	and since, like つ in H, ツ can also be used to double the following _____,	*situkoi* ("persistent")
743	エ ッ キ ス is read * _____,	consonant
744	and *gosikku* "Gothic" is written	*ekkisu* ("X" as in "X-ray" etc.; cf. *ekisu* "essence, extract")
745	The K sign for *te* is テ . Practice this in the usual way. → ⇉ テ *te* テ *te* テ *te*	ゴシック
746	K *te* is written	ー 二 テ *te* (etc.)

747	ステッキ is read *_____;	テ
748	and the K アイテ is written in H. □□□	*sutekki ("walking stick")
749	The K for *Tekisasu "Texas" is □□□	あいて (aite "companion, opponent")
750	and for *deeta "data" is □□	テキサス
751	and エキゾティック is read _____.	データ
752	K to is written ト . Copy and practice.	*ekizoteikku > *ekizotikku("exotic"; note the unusual kana spelling for the English "ti")

↓ト	to	ト	to	ト	to

753	エチケット is read *_____	├ ト to (etc.)
754	and *setto "(hair, tennis, film etc.) set" is written □□	*etiketto ("etiquette")
755	スカート is read *_____,	セット
756	トースト is read *_____;	*sukaato ("skirt")
757	カット is read *_____;	*toosuto ("toast")
758	and ジェット き (in which the last sign is in H because it is not part of the foreign word but a separate element meaning "machine, plane") is read *_____.	*katto ("woodcut, illustration")

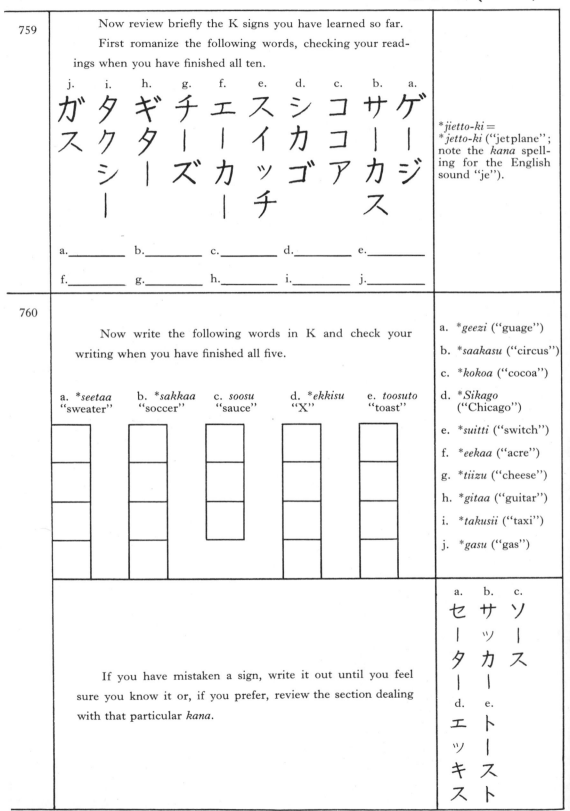

759

Now review briefly the K signs you have learned so far.

First romanize the following words, checking your readings when you have finished all ten.

j.　i.　h.　g.　f.　e.　d.　c.　b.　a.

ガ　タ　ギ　チ　エ　ス　シ　コ　サ　ゲ
ス　ク　タ　ー　ー　イ　カ　コ　ー　ー
シ　シ　ー　ズ　カ　ッ　ゴ　ア　カ　ジ
ー　　　　　　ー　チ　ッ　　　ス　ス
　　　　　　　　　チ

*jietto-ki =
*jetto-ki ("jet plane"; note the *kana* spelling for the English sound "je").

a.＿＿＿＿　b.＿＿＿＿　c.＿＿＿＿　d.＿＿＿＿　e.＿＿＿＿

f.＿＿＿＿　g.＿＿＿＿　h.＿＿＿＿　i.＿＿＿＿　j.＿＿＿＿

760

Now write the following words in K and check your writing when you have finished all five.

a. *seetaa*　b. *sakkaa*　c. *soosu*　d. *ekkisu*　e. *toosuto*
"sweater"　"soccer"　"sauce"　"X"　"toast"

a. *geezi* ("guage")

b. *saakasu* ("circus")

c. *kokoa* ("cocoa")

d. *Sikago* ("Chicago")

e. *suitti* ("switch")

f. *eekaa* ("acre")

g. *tiizu* ("cheese")

h. *gitaa* ("guitar")

i. *takusii* ("taxi")

j. *gasu* ("gas")

If you have mistaken a sign, write it out until you feel sure you know it or, if you prefer, review the section dealing with that particular *kana*.

a.　b.　c.
セ　サ　ソ
ー　ッ　ー
タ　カ　ス
ー　ー

d.　e.
エ　ト
ッ　ー
キ　ス
ス　ト

X. THE BASIC SIGNS: *na* to *mo*

Check your memory of the K signs already met by writing them against the corresponding H signs, as before.

1. た		2. す		3. あ		4. け		5. お	
6. え		7. ざ		8. ぎ		9. と		10. つ	
11. こ		12. せ		13. う		14. し		15. く	
16. い		17. か		18. ち		19. て		20. ぞ	

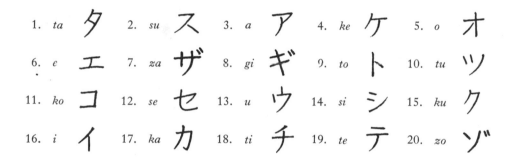

1. *ta* タ	2. *su* ス	3. *a* ア	4. *ke* ケ	5. *o* オ
6. *e* エ	7. *za* ザ	8. *gi* ギ	9. *to* ト	10. *tu* ツ
11. *ko* コ	12. *se* セ	13. *u* ウ	14. *si* シ	15. *ku* ク
16. *i* イ	17. *ka* カ	18. *ti* チ	19. *te* テ	20. *zo* ゾ

K na

761	The next sign is ナ which, coming after ト *to*, must be read ____.	
762	Practice writing ナ *na*. → ┌ ナ↓ *na* ナ *na* ナ *na*	*na*
763	シナ is read *_____.	ーナ *na* (etc.)
764	and カナダ is read *_____.	*Sina ("China")
765	The K for かたかな is	*Kanada ("Canada")

86

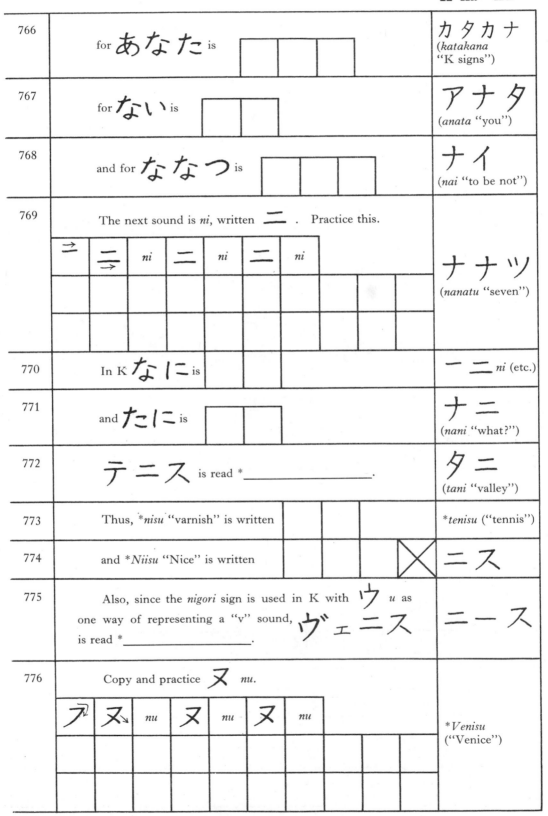

766	for あなた is [ ][ ][ ][ ]	カタカナ (*katakana* "K signs")
767	for ない is [ ][ ]	アナタ (*anata* "you")
768	and for ななつ is [ ][ ][ ]	ナイ (*nai* "to be not")
769	The next sound is *ni*, written ニ . Practice this. ⇉ ニ *ni* ニ *ni* ニ *ni*	ナナツ (*nanatu* "seven")
770	In K なに is	ー ニ *ni* (etc.)
771	and たに is [ ][ ]	ナ ニ (*nani* "what?")
772	テ ニ ス is read * _____ .	タ ニ (*tani* "valley")
773	Thus, *nisu* "varnish" is written	*tenisu* ("tennis")
774	and *Niisu* "Nice" is written	ニ ス
775	Also, since the *nigori* sign is used in K with ウ *u* as one way of representing a "v" sound, ヴェ ニ ス is read * _____ .	ニ ー ス
776	Copy and practice ヌ *nu*. ヌ *nu* ヌ *nu* ヌ *nu*	*Venisu* ("Venice")

777	In K いぬ is written [ ][ ][ ]	フ ヌ *nu* (etc.)
778	and きぬ is written [ ][ ][ ]	イ ヌ (*inu* "dog")
779	ヌード is read *______________;	キヌ (*kinu* "silk")
780	セーヌ is read *______________;	**nuudo* ("nude")
781	and **kanuu* "canoe" is written [ ][ ][ ][X]	**Seenu* ("Seine")
782	ス is read ____, and ヌ is read ____.	カヌー
783	If your answer to the above frame was right, jump to Frame 788. Remember that the second stroke cuts the first in [ ] *nu*,	*su*; *nu*
784	and supports it in [ ] *su*.	ヌ
785	Thus, in K ぬかす is [ ][ ][ ][X]	ス
786	Which, then, is *inu* "dog"? (a) イス (b) イヌ	ヌカス (*nukasu* "to omit")
787	What is the reading, then, of (a) イス ?	(b)
788	Learn now to write the K sign for *ne*: ネ ヽ フ ネ ネ *ne* ネ ネ ネ ネ *ne*	*isu* ("chair")
789	ネコ is read ______________;	ヽ ラ ネ ネ *ne* (etc.)
790	カネ is read ______________;	*neko* ("cat")

791	and ネヴァダ is read *_____ .	kane ("money")
792	The K for あね is [ ][ ][ ]	*Nevada ("Nevada")
793	and *Tenesii "Tennessee" is written [ ][ ][ ][ ]	ア ネ (ane "elder sister")
794	K no ノ has only one stroke. Practice this. ノ [no] ノ [no] ノ [no] [ ][ ][ ] [ ][ ][ ]	テ ネ シ ー
795	Do not confuse this sign, ノ no, with ソ —	ノ no (repeated)
796	Remember that, although both ノ and ソ are written downwards, no has _____ dot.	so
797	The K for そ の お と こ , then, is [ ][ ][ ][ ][ ]	no
798	としうえの is [ ][ ][ ][ ][ ]	ソノオトコ (sono otoko "that man")
799	and for としした の is [ ][ ][ ][ ][ ]	トシウエノ (tosiue no "older")
800	*Nooto "note (book)" is written [ ][ ][ ]	トシシタノ (tosisita no "younger")
801	and ノ ッ ト is read *_____ .	ノ ー ト
802	*Nokku "knock" is written [ ][ ][ ]	*notto ("nautical knot")
803	and ノ ッ ク ・ ア ウ ト is read *_____ .	ノ ッ ク

804	K *ha* is written ノ ハ. Copy and practice.	
	ノ| ノ ハ *ha* ノ ハ *ha* ノ ハ *ha*	*nokku-auto ("knock-out")

805	In K はは is written	ノ ノ ハ *ha* (etc.)
806	ハーグ is read *_____;	ノ ハ ノ ハ (*haha* "mother")
807	タバコ is read *_____;	*Haagu ("The Hague")
808	オートバイ is read *_____;	*tabako ("tobacco")
809	*basu* "bus" is written	*ootobai ("auto-motor-cycle")
810	*bataa* "butter" is written	バス
811	and *baketu* "bucket" is written	バター
812	The K signs for sounds with an initial *b* can also be used to write a foreign "v" sound. Thus, ノ バ is normally read *ba*; but it can also be used, like ヴァ , to represent the syllable __ __.	バケツ
813	For example, *Habana* "Havana"† is written	va

(†)   In romanizing, the following two principles have been observed:

1.   Where the *kana* is in accordance with traditional Japanese usage, it has been romanized directly, regardless of the foreign spelling, e.g. ハ ハ バ ナ *Habana*.

2.   Where the *kana* is a special combination used only for non-Japanese sounds, the foreign spelling has been taken into account, e.g. ハ ヴァ ナ *Havana*, and エ キ ゾ ティ ック (see Frame 751) > *ekizotikku*.

| 814 | and カ バ ー is read *_____. | ハ バ ナ |

815	Since the semi-voicing sign ○ is used to show an initial "p," as in H, アパート is read *_____ ;	*kabaa ("cover")
816	*pasu "pass" is written ☐☐	*apaato ("apartment [building], flats")
817	and *depaato "department store" is written ☐☐☐☐	パス
818	Like は in H, ハ is of course used to write the particle pronounced __ __.	デパート
819	Thus, the K for そのいぬには is ☐☐☐☐☐☐	wa
820	The K sign for hi is ヒ . Practice this. ⇥ ↓ヒ hi ヒ hi ヒ hi ☐☐☐☐ ☐☐☐☐	ソノイ ヌニハ (sono inu ni wa "on that dog")
821	コーヒー is read *_____ ;	ーヒ hi (etc.)
822	エチオピア is read *_____ ;	*koohii ("coffee")
823	and "Tahiti" is written in Japanese as ☐☐☐	*Etiopia ("Ethiopia")
824	*Saabisu "service" is written ☐☐☐	タヒチ
825	*piano "piano" is written ☐☐☐☐	サービス
826	and エービーシー is read *_____ .	ピアノ

827	The K sign for *hu* (*fu*) is フ . Learn this as usual.	
	フ | *hu* | フ | *hu* | フ | *hu* | | | |	*eebiisii* ("ABC")
828	ナイフ is read *_____;	フ *hu* (repeated)
829	フート is read *_____;	*naihu* ("knife")
830	and キエフ is read _____.	*huuto* ("foot [of measurement]")
831	As in the above examples, フ often corresponds to an English "f" or "fu" sound. When the "f" is followed by a vowel other than "u" (as in "*fastener*"), the sound can be represented by using フ for the "f" alone and following it by a small K sign for the appropriate vowel; e.g. "fa" is written ファ , and ファスナー is read _____.	*Kiehu* ("Kiev")
832	Similarly, フォーク is read *_____;	*fasunaa* ("[zip] fastener"; on the romanization *fa*, see second part of fn. to Frame 813)
833	ファシスト is read *_____;	*fooku* ("fork")
834	and *Okkusufoodo* "Oxford" is written	*fasisuto* ("Fascist")
835	Words using voiced forms of フ include: カーブ read *_____;	オックス フォード

836	*okutaabu "octave" written ⬚⬚⬚⬚⬚⬚	*kaabu ("curve")
837	スープ read *_____ ;	オクターブ
838	*paipu "pipe" written ⬚⬚⬚⬚	*suupu ("soup")
839	and *koppu "(wine, etc.)glass" written ⬚⬚⬚	パイプ
840	Note here that "cup (=trophy)" is カップ *_____.	コップ
841	The K sign for *he* is ∧ Practice this carefully, noting that the K sign has a sharper angle and is a shade smaller than H ∧ ⌃	*he*	∧	*he*	∧	*he*	 ⬚⬚⬚⬚⬚⬚⬚ ⬚⬚⬚⬚⬚⬚⬚	*kappu
842	Which of the following, then, are K signs? (a) ＼ (b) ＼ (c) ∧ (d) ⌃ (e) ∧	∧ *he* (repeated)
843	Now practice your own writing of the signs by copying them in the empty squares. 	H	K	H	K	H	K	K	K	H	K	 	∧	∧	∧	∧	∧	∧	∧	∧	∧	∧		(c) and (d)
844	ヘビー・ウェイト is read *_____ ;	
845	アベック is read *_____ ;	*hebii-weito (or *hebii-ueito, "heavy-weight")
846	*Tibetto "Tibet" is written ⬚⬚⬚⬚⬚	*abekku ("[unmarried] couple, lovers")
847	and *supeesu "space" is written ⬚⬚⬚⬚	チベット

848	Since an important use of the sign for *he*, in both H and K, is to write the particle _____ "to(wards),"	スペース
849	オトコハイエヘハ シッテイッタ is read _____,	*e*
850	and *Doitu e iku* "to go to Germany" is written in K ⬚⬚⬚⬚⬚⬚	*Otoko wa ie e hasitte itta* ("the man ran to the house")
851	The next sign is ホ . Being the sign for the last sound with an initial *h*, its reading is __ __.	ドイツヘ イク
852	Practice writing ホ *ho*. 一 ナ オ ホ *ho* ホ *ho* ホ *ho*	*ho*
853	アイダホ is read *_____;	一ナオホ *ho* (etc.)
854	ホット・ケーキ is read *_____;	*Aidaho* ("Idaho")
855	*aisu-hokkee* "ice-hockey" is written; ⬚⬚⬚⬚⬚⬚⬚⬚	*hotto-keeki* ("hotcake")
856	ボート is read *_____;	アイス・ ホッケー
857	and スポーツ is read *_____.	*booto* ("boat")
858	Note that オ *o* and ホ *ho* are somewhat similar; but you can keep them distinct because *ho* has MORE letters in its romanization and m_____ strokes in its *kana* sign.	*supootu* ("sport")

859	After the sounds beginning with *h* come those beginning with _____.	more
860	The first of these is *ma*, written マ in K.	*m*

ア	マ	ma	マ	ma	マ	ma			

861	マーケット is read *_____;	フ マ *ma* (etc.)
862	スマート is read *_____;	*maaketto* ("market")
863	and マッチ is read *_____.	*sumaato* ("smart")
864	*Panama* "Panama" is written [ ][ ][ ][✗]	*matti* ("match")
865	*teema* "theme, subject" is written	パナマ
866	and *paama* "permanent wave" is written [ ][ ][ ]	テーマ
867	イア・マーク is read*_____;	パーマ
868	and *ama* "amateur" is written [ ][ ][ ]	*ia-maaku* ("earmark")
869	Note that, although the first strokes of ア *a* and マ *ma* are very alike, the second strokes differ in length and direction. Practice these differences carefully below.	アマ

a	ma	a	ma	a	ma	a	ma	ma	ma
ア	マ	ア	マ	ア	マ	ア	マ	マ	マ

870	Practice writing ミ , the K sign for *mi*.							アマ (etc.)
	↘	ミ	ミ	*mi*	ミ	*mi*	ミ	*mi*

871	アカデミ is read *_____ ;	ˋ ˜ ミ *mi* (etc.)
872	ミシシッピ is read *_____ ;	*akademi ("academy")*
873	ミナ is read _____ ;	*Misisippi ("Mississippi")*
874	カミ is read _____ .	*mina ("all")*

875	In K *mina-sama* (respectful) "everyone" is written	*kami* ("god; paper; hair")
876	and *kami-sama* (respectful) "god" is written	ミナサマ

877	K *mu* is written ム . Practice this.					カミサマ
	↙	ム	*mu*	ム	*mu*	ム	*mu*

878	ゲーム is read *_____ ;	↙ ム *mu* (etc.)
879	チーム is read *_____ ;	*geemu ("game")*
880	ハム is read *_____ ;	*tiimu ("team")*
881	ゴム is read *_____ .	*hamu ("ham")*
882	and *egoizumu* "egoism" is written	*gomu ([<gum] "rubber")*

883	Do not confuse ム *mu* and マ ___	エゴイズム
884	Remember that [ma] *ma* has the same first stroke as the sign for its vowel *a*	*ma*
885	Thus, *makisimamu* "maximum" is written	マア
886	and *oobaa-taimu* "overtime" is written	マキシ マム
887	The K sign for *me* is メ . Copy and practice. リ メ *me* メ *me* メ *me*	オーバー・タイム ム
888	メキシコ is read *_____;	ノメ *me* (etc.)
889	メッカ is read *_____;	*Mekisiko ("Mexico")
890	*Meggu* "Meg" is written	*Mekka ("Mecca")
891	メー・デー is read *_____;	メッグ
892	and *kosumetikku* "cosmetics" is written	*Mee-dee ("May Day")
893	The final *m* sound, *mo*, is written モ in K. Practice this, noting that the vertical does not cut the top horizontal stroke, and that the order of strokes, too, is different from H *mo* も ⇒ ⇒ モ *mo* モ *mo* モ *mo*	コスメ チック

894	モスコー is read *_____;	ー ニ モ mo (etc.)
895	モットー is read *_____;	*Mosukoo ("Moscow")
896	kaimono "shopping" is written in K; ⬚⬚⬚⬚	*mottoo ("motto")
897	and the K for も う す is ⬚⬚⬚	カイモノ
898	for た て も の is ⬚⬚⬚⬚	モ ウ ス (moosu [humble] "to say"; remember that a straight line is used for long vowels only IN WESTERN WORDS).
899	and for も も is ⬚⬚	タ テ モ ノ (tatemono "building")
900	Now that you have met most of the K signs, test your memory of them by transcribing the sentences below into or from K, checking each one as you go. うえのへいきますか。 ⬚⬚⬚⬚⬚⬚⬚⬚⬚⬚⬚	モ モ (momo "peach")
901	いったことのないいせ。 ⬚⬚⬚⬚⬚⬚⬚⬚⬚⬚⬚	ウエノヘイ キマスカ。 (Ueno e ikimasu ka "Will you go to Ueno ?")
902	けいさつとはなしても。 ⬚⬚⬚⬚⬚⬚⬚⬚⬚⬚⬚	イッタコト ノナイイセ。 (Itta koto no nai Ise "Ise where I have never been")
903	あなたのまえのこいぬ。 ⬚⬚⬚⬚⬚⬚⬚⬚⬚⬚	ケイサツト ハナシテモ。 (Keisatu to hanasite mo "Even if you talk to the police")

904	そのへいたいはいつふね にいましたか。	アナタノマ エノコイヌ (*Anata no mae no koinu* "The puppy in front of you")
905	かみのけのあかいひと。	ソノヘイタイハイツフネニイマシタカ。 (*Sono heitai wa itu hune ni imasita ka* "When was that soldier in the ship?")
906	ちもにくもないほねは。	カミノケノ アカイヒト。 (*Kami-no-ke no akai hito* "A person with red hair")
907	ヒノタメニアツイガッコウ。	チモニクモ ナイホネハ。 (*Ti mo niku mo nai hone wa* "The bone with neither blood nor meat")
908	アノタテモノニスムトオモイマス。	*Hi no tame ni atui gakkoo* ("A school hot because of the sun")
909	チカクノヒトノイウコトニツイテキク。	*Ano tatemono ni sumu to omoimasu* ("I think he will live in that house")
	If you mistook a *kana* sign once only in the above ten examples, write it out WITH ITS READING (e.g. マ *ma*) until you are sure you know it. If you mistook the same *kana* sign more than once, review the section in which it was introduced. Then continue with the next section.	*Tikaku no hito no yuu koto ni tuite kiku* ("To ask about what the local people say")

XI. THE BASIC SIGNS : *ya* to *n*

First, check the K signs already learned by transcribing the following H signs, as before.

1. せ	2. ど	3. き	4. ね	5. ち	6. え	7. さ
8. う	9. ば	10. ぺ	11. に	12. も	13. だ	14. す
15. が	16. み	17. い	18. ぬ	19. し	20. ぷ	21. く
22. め	23. ひ	24. て	25. お	26. む	27. あ	28. の
29. ご	30. ま	31. げ	32. つ	33. そ	34. ほ	35. な

1. *se* セ   2. *do* ド   3. *ki* キ   4. *ne* ネ   5. *ti* チ   6. *e* エ   7. *sa* サ

8. *u* ウ   9. *ba* バ   10. *pe* ペ   11. *ni* ニ   12. *mo* モ   13. *da* ダ   14. *su* ス

15. *ga* ガ   16. *mi* ミ   17. *i* イ   18. *nu* ヌ   19. *si* シ   20. *pu* プ   21. *ku* ク

22. *me* メ   23. *hi* ヒ   24. *te* テ   25. *o* オ   26. *mu* ム   27. *a* ア   28. *no* ノ

29. *go* ゴ   30. *ma* マ   31. *ge* ゲ   32. *tu* ツ   33. *so* ソ   34. *ho* ホ   35. *na* ナ

K ya

910	The first of the three initial-*y* sounds, *ya*, is written ヤ in K. Practice this in the usual way.	
	ヤ	*ya*	ヤ	*ya*	ヤ	*ya*		

911	Contrast it with the rounder, fuller H sign や by writing both signs in the empty squares below.	⁀ヤ
H	K	H	K	H	K	H	K	K	K	*ya* (etc.)
や	ヤ	や	ヤ	や	ヤ	や	ヤ	ヤ	ヤ	

912	タイヤ is read *_____;	やヤ (etc.)
913	ギヤ is read *_____;	*taiya ("tyre")
914	"Asia" is written as *Aziya* [ ][ ][ ] or, alternatively, as *Azia* [ ][ ]	*giya ("gear")
915	and similarly "Ethiopia" is written as *Etiopiya* [ ] [ ][ ][ ] or as *Etiopia* [ ][ ][ ]	アジヤ アジア
916	The Japanese word for "piano" can be either *piano* ピアノ or, alternatively, *piyano* [ ][ ][ ]	エチオピヤ エチオピア
917	Similarly, ピアニスト meaning "_____,"	ピヤノ
918	has the alternative form [ ][ ][ ][ ][ ][✕]	"pianist"
919	Since, as we saw, the three syllables *ya*, *yu* and *yo* are much used to form diphthongs, シャツ is read *_____;	ピヤニスト
920	ジャケツ is read *_____;	*syatu ("vest, singlet")
921	and *zyaketto* "book jacket" is written [ ][ ][ ][ ][ ]	*zyaketu ("sweater, jersey")
922	Moreover, in writing Western words, a short "ka" sound is often transcribed as the diphthong *kya*. For example, キャベツ is *_____ "cabbage,"	ジャケット
923	and "cabinet" is written *kyabine* [ ][ ][ ][ ]	*kyabetu

924	The K sign for *yu* is ユ . Practice this.	キャビネ

プ	ユ →	*yu*	ユ	*yu*	ユ	*yu*			

925	Keep it distinct from コ *ko*, in which the bottom line must NOT extend to the right of the vertical. Practice the two signs a few times.	７ ユ *yu* (etc.)

ko	*yu*	*ko*	*yu*	*ko*	*yu*	*yu*	*yu*
コ	ユ	コ	ユ	コ	ユ	ユ	ユ

926	Thus, オ ユ is read _____;	コ ユ (etc.)
927	ユ ミ is read _____;	*o-yu* ("hot water")
928	and in K ゆ め is written ▢ ▢ ▢	*yumi* ("bow" [weapon])
929	In most of the foreign words in which it is used, however, *yu* forms part of a diphthong: ジュース is read *_____;	ユ メ (*yume* "dream")
930	ア マ チュ ア is read *_____;	*zyuusu* ("juice")
931	*sutyuadesu* "stewardess" is written ▢▢▢▢▢▢	*amatyua* ("amateur")
932	ポ タ ー ジュ is read *_____;	ス チュ ア デ ス
933	and *Masatyuusettu* "Massachusetts" is written ▢▢▢▢▢▢▢	*potaazyu* ("[thick] soup")

934	Do not forget, however, that the romanization of the verb *yuu* "to say" is irregular, its *kana* spelling being う or ウ	マサチュー セッツ
935	K *yo* is written ヨ . Practice this. ヲ ヨ ヨ *yo* ヨ *yo* ヨ *yo*	い；イ
936	ヨット is read *＿＿＿＿＿＿＿＿ ;	フ ヲ ヨ *yo* (etc.)
937	チョーク is read *＿＿＿＿＿＿＿＿ ;	*yotto* ("yacht")
938	*Yookusiya* "Yorkshire" is written	*tyooku* ("chalk")
939	*Nyuu Yooku* "New York" is written	ヨーク シャ
940	and the K for よのなか is	ニュー・ ヨーク
941	K *ra* is written ラ . Copy and practice. ラ *ra* ラ *ra* ラ *ra*	ヨノナカ (*yo-no-naka* "the world, society")
942	ラジオ is read *＿＿＿＿＿＿ ;	ˉ ラ *ra* (etc.)
943	ブラシ is read *＿＿＿＿＿ ;	*razio* ("radio")
944	ラグビー is read *＿＿＿＿＿＿ ;	*burasi* ("brush")

| 945 | *garasu "(plate) glass" is written | | | | ☒ | *ragubii ("rugby") |

| 946 | タイプライター is read *_____ ; | ガラス |

| 947 | *kasutera "sponge-cake" is written | *taipuraitaa ("typewriter") |

| 948 | and *kamera "camera" (one of the few words in which a short English initial "ka" sound becomes simply カ instead of キャ) is written | カステラ |

| 949 | Now practice writing K ri | カメラ |

↓ | リ↓ | ri | リ | ri | リ | ri

| 950 | Contrast this with H ri り , which, as in similar cases, is less straight and stiff.   Practice the two signs. | リ リ ri (etc.) |

H	K	H	K	H	K	H	K	H	K
り	リ	り	リ	り	リ	り	リ	り	リ

| 951 | アメリカ is read *_____ ; | り リ (etc.) |

| 952 | イギリス is read *_____ ; | *Amerika ("America") |

| 953 | *Parii "Paris" is written | *Igirisu ("England, Great Britain") |

| 954 | and *Kirisuto "Christ" is written | | | ☒ | パリー |

955	Beware of two words which do not mean what an English speaker might assume: ブリキ read *_____ means "tin-plate";	キリスト
956	and シュー・クリーム read *_____,means a "cream puff."	*buriki
957	The K sign for ru is ル . Copy and practice. ノ↓ ル↓ ru ル ru ル ru	*syuu-kuriimu
958	テーブル is read *_____;	ノ ル ru (etc.)
959	メートル is read *_____;	*teeburu ("table")
960	ゴルフ is read *_____;	*meetoru("metre")
961	and アルコール is read *_____.	*goruhu ("golf")
962	Incidentally, the word for the alcoholic drink *biiru "beer" [ ][ ][ ] also has a long vowel,	*arukooru ("alcohol")
963	and this distinguishes it from *biru "building" [ ][ ]	ビール
964	*Hoteru "(Western-type) hotel" is written [ ][ ]	ビル
965	*puuru "swimming-pool" is written [ ][ ][ ]	ホテル

966	アルバイト is read *_____;	プール
967	and オールド・ミス is read *_____.	*arubaito ("spare-time work")
968	Practice writing K re レ レ | re | レ | re | レ | re	*oorudo-misu ("old maid")
969	レコード is read *_____;	レ re (repeated)
970	エレベーター is read *_____;	*rekoodo ("record")
971	*Tyokoreeto "chocolate" is written	*erebeetaa ("elevator, lift")
972	*koohii-bureiku "coffee break" is written	チョコ レート
973	トイレット or simply トイレ will be read _____ (tto);	コーヒー・ ブレイク
974	and マレー is read *_____.	*toire (tto) ("toilet")
975	ロ is the K sign for ro. Practice this. ロ | ro | ロ | ro | ロ | ro	*Maree ("Malaya")

976	ヨーロッパ is read *_____;	イ ワ ロ *ro* (etc.)
977	カイロ is read *_____;	* *Yooroppa* ("Europe")
978	*ero* is a common abbreviation for *erotisizumu* "eroticism," written ☐☐☐☐☐☐☐	**Kairo* ("Cairo")
979	*maikuro-ueebu* "micro-wave" is written ☐☐☐☐☐☐☐☐☐	エロチ シズム
980	プロレタリヤ is read *_____;	マイクロ・ ウエーブ
981	and **Osuroo* "Oslo" is written ☐☐☐☐☒	**puroretariya* ("proletariat")
982	The first sound with an initial "*w*" is *wa*, written ワ in K. Write this out with its reading several times. ↓ ワ *wa* ワ *wa* ワ *wa* ☐☐☐☐ ☐☐☐☐	オスロー
983	The sound *wa* is always written with this sign in K, unless of course it is the particle *wa*, when it is written ☐	イ ワ *wa* (etc.)
984	In K, therefore, *hanawa wa* "(as for) the wreath" is written ☐☐☐☐	ハ
985	**Hawai* "Hawaii" is written ☐☐☐☒	ハナワハ
986	**Warusoo* "Warsaw" is written ☐☐☐☐	ハワイ
987	**waisyatu* "shirt" is written ☐☐☐☐	ワルソー

988	and オーバー・ワーク is read * _____.	ワイシャツ
989	Note that ワ is ___ , and ウ is ____ .	
990	If your answers were correct, omit this and the next two frames. If you confused the two signs, remember that *wa* can mean "wheel" and that, like a wheel, [ ] *wa* has no projections.	*wa* ; *u*
991	Thus, in K *uwasa* "rumor, gossip" is written [ ][ ][ ]	ワ
992	and *warau* "to laugh" is written [ ][ ][ ][X]	ウワサ
993	K *(w)i* is written 井 . It is little used now, but practice writing it so that you will readily recognize it. → / ㇐ エ 井↓ *(w)i* 井 *(w)i* 井 *(w)i*	ワラウ
994	The modern simplified system of writing officially ignores the signs ゐ and 井 , and uses instead the signs [ ] and [ ] for the simple vowel *i*.	一 ㇐ エ 井 *(w)i* (etc.)
995	Hence, *iru* "to be," formerly written with a 井 in K, is now written [ ][ ]	い ; イ
996	and *kurai* "degree, extent," also formerly written with a 井 in K, is now written [ ][ ][ ]	イル
997	(*W*)*e* has similarly been replaced by ____ .	クライ

| 998 | Practice writing (w)e too, so that you will immediately recognize it.

(Remember that (w)e **ヱ** has a little more in it than e **エ** .) | *e* |

	⇒	ヱ↓	ヱ⇒	(w)e	ヱ	(w)e	ヱ	(w)e		

| 999 | *E* "picture," for example, which used to be written **ヱ** in K, is now written [ ] | ⁷ ア ヱ
(w)e (etc.) |

| 1,000 | and *koe* "voice," which also used to be written with a **ヱ** in K, is now written [ ][ ] | **エ** |

| 1,001 | Practice carefully the writing of **ヲ** (w)o, the last sign for a combined consonant and vowel sound. | **コ エ** |

	⇒	⹀⇒	ヲ↓	(w)o	ヲ	(w)o	ヲ	(w)o		

| 1,002 | Distinguish **ヲ** (w)o from **ラ** ra: unlike ra **ラ** (w)o **ヲ** is written in three strokes, and has the downstroke starting from the top horizontal.

Practice the two signs. | ⁻ ⁼ ヲ
(w)o (etc.) |

ra	(w)o	ra	(w)o	ra	(w)o	ra	(w)o	(w)o
ラ	ヲ	ラ	ヲ	ラ	ヲ	ラ	ヲ	ヲ

1,003	Except when it is used to write the accusative particle *o*, (*w*)*o* too is now normally replaced by the simple vowel. Thus, in all uses but one, ヲ is replaced by [ ]	ラ ヲ (etc.)
1,004	*Sao* "pole," then, which used to be written with a ヲ in K, is now written [ ][ ]	オ
1,005	and *otoko* "man," which also used to be written with a ヲ in K, is now written [ ][ ][ ]	サ オ
1,006	But, since the sign for (*w*)*o* is still used for the accusative particle *o*, カ シ ヲ カ ウ is read _____ ;	オ ト コ
1,007	and in K こ し を か け る is written [ ][ ][ ][ ][ ][ ]	*kasi o kau* ("to buy cakes")
1,008	The last basic K sign is ン for *n*. Practice this carefully, noting that it is written in much the same way as シ *si*, but with only one short stroke before the long upward one.	コ シ ヲ カ ケ ル *(kosi o kakeru* "to sit down")
1,009	Distinguish ン *n* from ソ *so*: in the latter the long stroke is rounder and written _____ wards.	ヽ ン *n* (etc.)
1,010	Practice the two signs together until your writing makes them quite distinct.	down

1,008 practice row:

	n		*n*		*n*		*n*
ン	ン		ン		ン		

1,010 practice row:

n	*so*	*n*	*so*	*n*	*so*	*n*	*so*	*n*	*n*
ン	ソ	ン	ソ	ン	ソ	ン	ソ	ン	ン

1,011	Now transcribe the following works to or from K, as appropriate. セメント *_____	ン ソ (etc.)
1,012	ズボン *_____	*semento ("cement")
1,013	カバン *_____	*zubon ("trousers")
1,014	*botan "button" ☐☐☐☐	*kaban ("case, trunk")
1,015	*hanketi "handkerchief" ☐☐☐☐ ⊠	ボタン
1,016	*Huransu "France" ☐☐☐ ⊠	ハンケチ
1,017	*sutokkingu "stocking" ☐☐☐☐☐☐☐	フ ラ ン ス
1,018	サ ラ リ ー マ ン *_____	ストッキ ング
1,019	and *akusento "accent" ☐☐☐☐☐☐	*sarariiman("white-collar worker")
		アクセント

KATAKANA TEST SENTENCES

Now that you have covered all the K signs, test yourself by transcribing the following sentences completely into K. Then check with the transcriptions given at the bottom of the page and relearn any *kana* you have wrong.

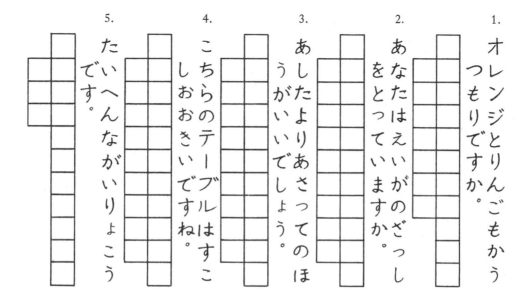

5. たいへんながいりょこうです。

4. こちらのテーブルはすこしおおきいですね。

3. あしたよりあさってのほうがいいでしょう。

2. あなたはえいがのざっしをとっていますか。

1. オレンジとりんごもかうつもりですか。

5. タイヘンナガイリョコウデス。

4. コチラノテーブルハスコシオオキイデスネ。

3. アシタヨリアサッテノホウガイイデショウ。

2. アナタハエイガノザッシヲトッテイマスカ。

1. オレンジトリンゴモカウツモリデスカ。

(1. *Orenzi to ringo mo kau tumori desu ka.*
"Do you intend to buy oranges and apples too?")

(2. *Anata wa eiga no zassi o totte imasu ka.*
"Do you take a film magazine?")

(3. *Asita yori asatte no hoo ga ii desyoo.*
"The day after tomorrow would probably be better than tomorrow")

(4. *Kotira no teeburu wa sukosi ookii desu ne.*
"This table over here is a bit big, isn't it?")

(5. *Taihen nagai ryokoo desu.*
"It is a very long journey")

XII. FOREIGN WORDS IN JAPANESE

This short final section brings together some general points about the use of foreign words in Japanese.

Having met many words always written in K (those marked with*), you have also met most of the peculiarities of the K spellings of foreign words. These peculiarities arise, of course, from the basic difficulty of representing a wide range of foreign sounds by means of a limited number of phonetic signs devised only for the sounds of Japanese. When faced with an unusual sound or combination of sounds in a Western word, an educated Japanese can usually imitate it well enough in his own speech; but when he comes to write the word in Japanese, all that he can do is to use the *kana*, singly or in combination, which come closest to the sounds he hears. Thus, foreign words appear even more changed in their Japanese written forms than they do when used in Japanese speech. (Do not feel you have made a mistake, therefore, if you fail to identify the original foreign words from their *kana* spellings in the frames below.)

1,020	For example, the transcription of "lens" as **renzu*	
1,021	illustrates how an "l" sound has to be written as an ___ sound in Japanese;	レンズ
1,022	how an "n" can be written with/without difficulty;	r
1,023	but how other consonants such as "s" have to be written with *kana* signs for a consonant + ________________.	without
1,024	Also, an English "th" sound is not found in Japanese; and when unvoiced it is usually written as an initial *-s* sound: スリル is *____________ "____________";	vowel
1,025	and when voiced, as an initial-*z* sound: ギャザー is *____________ "(sewn) gathers."	**suriru* "thrill"
1,026	A "hu" ("hoo") or "fu" ("foo") sound is written as フ, lengthened where necessary: フード *____________ "hood";	**gyazaa*

1,027	フットボール * _____ "football."	*huudo
1,028	An "f" sound followed by a vowel other than "u" is written as フ plus a sign for the appropriate vowel: ファン * _____ " _____ ";	*huttobooru
1,029	フェア・プレー * _____ " _____ "	*fan ("fan [=admirer")
1,030	The short English "ka" sound as in "cat" (or "ga" sound as in "gaberdine") is usually written キャ (or ギャ). "Gathers," as we saw above, is written *gyazaa □□□□	*fea-puree ("fair play")
1,031	and キャンプ is read * _____ " _____."	ギャザー
1,032	The English word "camera" is unusual in now being written simply as □□□	*kyanpu ("camp")
1,033	Usually the plain カ is reserved for the short English "u" sound, as in "cut": カット is * _____.	カメラ
1,034	Similarly, パ usually represents the English "pu" sound, as in パテ * _____ " _____."	*katto ("[wood] cut, illustration")
1,035	In kana the guttural "ch" sound found in "loch" etc. is shown by a small ツ before the sign for the initial "h" sound which echoes the preceding vowel. In writing "Bach," for example, the initial "h" sound used is "ha," to match the vowel in the preceding "ba." Thus, "Bach" is spelled in K as ba+tu+ha. □□□	*pate ("putty")
1,036	"van Gogh," then, uses ho and is written ファン・ □□□	バッハ

1,037	and "Zurich" is written チュー	✕	ゴッホ
1,038	The Japanese like to use foreign words, and the only restriction is the understanding of the hearer or reader. 　Any foreign word can be used in Japanese provided it is under＿＿＿＿＿＿＿＿.		（チュー） リッヒ
1,039	Some foreign words are, of course, much more commonly used than others; and most of these words have generally accepted *kana* spellings. 　There are usually standard *kana* spellings for the more com＿＿＿＿＿ foreign words.		understood
1,040	But, since *kana* does not represent foreign sounds very exactly, there is sometimes more than one way of showing the same sound. 　The same sound may be written in K in d ＿＿＿＿＿ ent ways.		common
1,041	Such inconsistencies are to be found even in the standard *kana* spellings of common foreign words. 　For example, the Japanese word for "beer" is *biiru* 		different
1,042	but "beer-hall" is *biya-hooru* 		ビール
1,043	Again, the English short "ti" sound is generally written as チ , as in チップ *＿＿＿＿ "＿＿＿＿";		ビヤ・ ホール
1,044	but, as we saw, it becomes テ in ステッキ *＿＿＿＿＿＿ "＿＿＿＿＿."		*tippu* "tip(=gratuity)"
1,045	and ティ in エキゾティック *＿＿＿＿＿＿＿ "＿＿＿＿＿＿";		*sutekki* "(walking) stick"
1,046	Sometimes, in fact, there are perfectly acceptable alternative K spellings for foreign words. 　A long "ti" sound (as in "par*ty*") is usually ティー and, hence, a long "di" sound is usually		*ekizotikku* "exotic"

1,047	For example, "party" is *paatii	ディー
1,048	and "parody" is *parodii	パー ティー
1,049	But both スティール and スチール are found for the English word "_____."	パロ ディー
1,050	Then, too, both スチュー and シチュー are found for "_____";	"steel"
1,051	and both イア and イヤ are found for the English "ia" combination. Thus, "Ethiopia" may be either ア or	"stew"
1,052	The sound "je," too, is often written either as je ジェ as we saw in ジェットき *_____ "_____,"	エチオピア エチオピヤ
1,053	or as ze ゼ "Jelly," for example, can be either *jerii	*jetto-ki "jet plane"
1,054	or *zerii	ジェリー
1,055	and "gesture" can be either *jesutyaa	ゼリー
1,056	or *zesutyaa	ジェス チャー

1,057	Finally, you have seen also how there are two ways of representing a "v" sound in Japanese. It can either be written with the appropriate sign for *ba, bi, bu, be* or *bo*, as in サービス for the English word "_____";	ゼス チャー
1,058	or, as in ヴィクトリア "_____"	"service"
1,059	it can be shown by the use of the sign □□	"Victoria"
1,060	Thus, it is not surprising to find in the same music program both バイオリン *_____ "_____."	ヴ
1,061	and ヴィオラ *_____ "_____."	*baiorin* "violin"
1,062	Such unfixed spellings are comparatively few, but there are two general points which the English-speaking student of Japanese should bear in mind. The first is the obvious one that, although most of the foreign words used in Japanese are English, the language has also borrowed a number of words from other sources and, in general, pronounces them accordingly. We find, for example, *Uiin □□□□ for "Vienna,"	*viora* "viola"
1,063	*enerugii □□□□□ for "energy,"	ウィーン
1,064	*zyanru □□□ for "genre,"	エネルギー
1,065	and *Rooma □□□ for "Rome."	ジャンル
1,066	"Italy" can similarly be *Itariya □□□□	ローマ
1,067	but the English version *Itarii □□□□ is now rather more usual.	イタリヤ

1,068	There is no particular difficulty about such words, provided they are recognized as not being of English origin. We saw, for example, that it would not do to assume that シュー・クリーム *_____ "_____" was a direct borrowing from English.	イタリー
1,069	The other general point is that a loan word, whether from English or another language, does not always appear in the form or meaning one might expect. The Japanese version of "London," for instance, did not become ランダン , but followed the spelling as *Rondon	*syuu-kuriimu "cream puff"
1,070	"ink" is not *inku* (on the lines of "tank" = *tanku* タンク) but *inki*	ロンドン
1,071	the German word *arbeit* "work" has been taken into Japanese as *arubaito* with the more limited meaning of "*spare-time* work";	インキ
1,072	and *pudingu* is used to mean, not "pudding" in general, but "baked custard (pudding)."	アルバイト
1,073	You must also be flexible in the reliance you place on the use of the solid dot • to separate words, etc. within a foreign phrase. Usually it is reliable and a help in recognizing the original phrase: クローズ・アップ *_____ "_____";	プディング
1,074	ヒット・ナンバー *_____ "_____."	*kuroozu-appu "close-up"

1,075	But sometimes it is unhelpful, either through an unexpected division of the original: ショーマン・シップ * _____ " _____ ";	*hitto-nanbaa* "hit number"
1,076	or because of the limitations of *kana* itself: フェタ・コンプリ * _____ " _____ "	*syooman-sippu* "showmanship"
1,077	Even more disconcerting to a foreigner can be the common Japanese habit of shortening a foreign word after adoption. "Department (store)," for example, becomes *depaato*	*feta-konpuri* "fait accompli"
1,078	and, similarly, "apartment (building)" becomes *apaato*	デパート
1,079	"overcoat" becomes *oobaa*	アパート
1,080	"puncture" becomes *panku*	オーバー
1,081	テレビ is used for テレビジョン " _____ ";	パンク
1,082	スト is used for ストライキ " _____ ";	"television"
1,083	デモ is used for デモンストレーション " _____ ";	"strike"
1,084	and コネ is used for コネクション " _____ ."	"demonstration"

1,085	Sometimes the abbreviation can confuse identification either by itself looking like another word: サンド for example, is short for サンドイッチ "_____";	"connection (=influence, "pull")"
1,086	or by being used for more than one longer word: センチ for example, can be short for either センチメンタル "_____";	"sandwich"
1,087	or for センチメートル "_____"	"sentimental"
1,088	and the full words for which the shortened form プロ is used include プロレタリヤ "_____"	"centimetre"
1,089	プログラム "_____"	"proletariat"
1,090	プロダクション "_____"	"program"
1,091	and プロフェッショナル "_____"	"production (=film studio)"
1,092	In the combination プロ・レス however, it can have only the last meaning, for レス too is an abbreviation, and the whole phrase is short for—what, do you think? "_____ _____"	"professional"
	Now that you have covered all the *kana* and their combinations used in the modern written language, make sure that you remember them all by working through the review of the signs on the next page. Then, when you feel that you know them all individually, try the final test in which they are used in complete sentences.	"professional wrestling"

Appendix 1
REVIEW OF KANA

Write both the H and K for each of the following sounds in the squares provided. When you have finished them all, check what you have written with the answers at the bottom of the page and relearn thoroughly any sign you had wrong.

To help you with this, the number of the page on which each basic sign (that is, the unvoiced sign, e.g. か for が) was introduced is given below the sign in question.

1. sa	2. mo	3. a	4. da	5. mi	6. ke	7. ha	8. ru	9.(w)e	10. ho
11. te	12. yu	13. ka	14. he	15. no	16. u	17. ti	18. wa	19. me	20. re
21. ya	22. si	23. i	24. na	25. ri	26. to	27. mu	28. se	29. go	30.(w)i
31. su	32. ma	33. hu	34. nu	35. ku	36. yo	37. hi	38. o	39. ro	40. n
41. e	42. ne	43. ki	44. tu	45. ra	46. ni	47.(w)o	48. pu	49. bo	50. so

1. sa	2. mo	3. a	4. da	5. mi	6. ke	7. ha	8. ru	9.(w)e	10. ho
さ / サ	も / モ	あ / ア	だ / ダ	み / ミ	け / ケ	は / ハ	る / ル	ゑ / エ	ほ / ホ
27 / 76	46 / 96	19 / 69	31 / 80	44 / 95	25 / 74	39 / 89	51 / 104	55 / 108	42 / 93
11. te	12. yu	13. ka	14. he	15. no	16. u	17. ti	18. wa	19. me	20. re
て / テ	ゆ / ユ	か / カ	へ / ヘ	の / ノ	う / ウ	ち / チ	わ / ワ	め / メ	れ / レ
34 / 82	49 / 101	23 / 72	41 / 92	39 / 88	21 / 70	31 / 80	53 / 106	45 / 96	52 / 105
21. ya	22. si	23. i	24. na	25. ri	26. to	27. mu	28. se	29. go	30.(w)i
や / ヤ	し / シ	い / イ	な / ナ	り / リ	と / ト	む / ム	せ / セ	ご / ゴ	ゐ / ヰ
49 / 99	28 / 77	20 / 70	37 / 85	51 / 103	34 / 83	44 / 95	30 / 78	25 / 74	54 / 107
31. su	32. ma	33. hu	34. nu	35. ku	36. yo	37. hi	38. o	39. ro	40. n
す / ス	ま / マ	ふ / フ	ぬ / ヌ	く / ク	よ / ヨ	ひ / ヒ	お / オ	ろ / ロ	ん / ン
29 / 77	43 / 94	41 / 91	38 / 86	24 / 73	50 / 102	40 / 90	22 / 71	52 / 105	56 / 109
41. e	42. ne	43. ki	44. tu	45. ra	46. ni	47.(w)o	48. pu	49. bo	50. so
え / エ	ね / ネ	き / キ	つ / ツ	ら / ラ	に / ニ	を / ヲ	ぷ / プ	ぼ / ボ	そ / ソ
21 / 71	38 / 87	24 / 73	32 / 81	51 / 102	37 / 86	55 / 108	41 / 91	42 / 93	30 / 79

Appendix 2
FINAL TEST

Transcribe the first section, 1—6, into *kana* (i.e. into H, with K where appropriate), and then the second section, 7—11, into roman letters.

As you finish each section, check with the correct versions given underneath and count up your *different* mistakes (wrong type of *kana*, wrong *kana* sign or spelling etc.), ignoring repetitions of what is essentially the same mistake.

1. *Anata no tomodati wa mada Amerika ni imasu ka.*
   "Is your friend still in America?"

2. *Ie, moo Yooroppa e ryokoo site imasu.*
   "No, he is now on a journey to Europe."

3. *Watasi no hako no naka ni nani ka haitte imasu ka.*
   "Is there something inside my box?"

4. *E, retaa-peepaa mo pen mo inki mo haitte imasu.*
   "Yes, there is some writing paper, a pen and some ink in it."

5. *Asoko de taipuraitaa o tukatte iru no wa neesan desyoo?*
   "I believe that is your elder sister using the typewriter over there?"

6. *Ginza no supootu no mise de yumi to ya o tyuumon site kimasita.*
   "I have been to order a bow and some arrows at a sports shop on the Ginza."

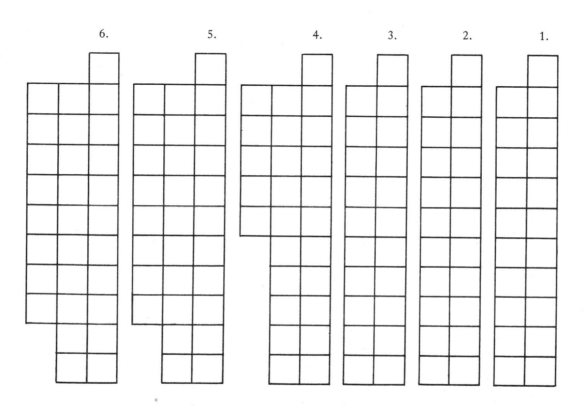

1. あなたのともだちはまだアメリカにいますか。

2. いえ、もうヨーロッパへりょこうしています。

3. わたしのはこのなかにないにかはいっていますか。

4. え、レター・ペーパーもペンもインキもはいっています。

5. あそこでタイプライターをつかっているのはねえさんでしょう。

6. ぎんざのスポーツのみせでゆみとやをちゅうもんしてきました。

7. あそこになにがありますか。いすとテーブルがあります。

8. いすはいくつありますか。よっつあります。

9. テーブルはいくつありますか。ふたつあります。

10. そこにフォークがいくつありますか。むっつあります。

11. ナイフもむっつありますか。ナイフはなっつあります。

7. _____

8. _____

9. _____

10. _____

11. _____

7. *Asoko ni nani ga arimasu ka.   Isu to teeburu ga arimasu.*
   ("What is there over there?"   "Chairs and tables.")

8. *Isu wa ikutu arimasu ka.   Yottu arimasu.*
   ("How many chairs are there?"   "There are four.")

9. *Teeburu wa ikutu arimasu ka.   Hutatu arimasu.*
   ("How many tables are there?"   "There are two.")

10. *Soko ni fooku ga ikutu arimasu ka.   Muttu arimasu.*
    ("How many forks do you have there?"   "Six.")

11. *Naihu mo muttu arimasu ka.   Naihu wa nanatu arimasu.*
    ("Are there six knives too?"   "There are seven knives.")

If you learned and relearned the *kana* at each stage as directed, you should have had very few, if any, mistakes.   A total of more than ten different mistakes for the whole test means that you should spend some time learning thoroughly all the *kana* or combinations of *kana* you had wrong.

Appendix 3
HIRAGANA

	A あ	I い	U う	E え	O お		*Voiced Sounds*				
K	ka か	ki き	ku く	ke け	ko こ	→	ga が	gi ぎ	gu ぐ	ge げ	go ご
S	sa さ	si (shi) し	su す	se せ	so そ	→	za ざ	zi (ji) じ	zu ず	ze ぜ	zo ぞ
T	ta た	ti (chi) ち	tu (tsu) つ	te て	to と	→	da だ	zi (ji) ぢ	zu づ	de で	do ど
N	na な	ni に	nu ぬ	ne ね	no の		ba ば	bi び	bu ぶ	be べ	bo ぼ
H	ha は	hi ひ	hu (fu) ふ	he へ	ho ほ		pa ぱ	pi ぴ	pu ぷ	pe ぺ	po ぽ
M	ma ま	mi み	mu む	me め	mo も						
Y	ya や		yu ゆ		yo よ						
R	ra ら	ri り	ru る	re れ	ro ろ						
W	wa わ	(w)i ゐ		(w)e ゑ	(w)o を						
N final ん											

Long Vowels (Follow the romanization except usually for *oo*)			
aa あ あ	*kaa* か あ	*baa* ば あ	etc.
ii い い	*tii* ち い	*mii* み い	etc.
uu う う	*guu* ぐ う	*suu* す う	etc.
ee え え	*nee* ね え	*mee* め え	etc.
oo お う	*koo* こ う	*too* と う	etc. (but

お お and こ お and と お in *ooi* "many,"
oo- "big," *koori* "ice," *tooru* "to pass along"
and related words)

Diphthongs					
Short Vowels (*ki* etc. + *ya, yu* or *yo*)			Long Vowels (*kyu, kyo* etc. + *u*)		
kya き ゃ	*sya* し ゃ	etc.	———————	———————	
kyu き ゅ	*syu* し ゅ	etc.	*kyuu* き ゅ う	*syuu* し ゅ う	etc.
kyo き ょ	*syo* し ょ	etc.	*kyoo* き ょ う	*syoo* し ょ う	etc.

Appendix 4
KATAKANA

	A ア	I イ	U ウ	E エ	O オ		*Voiced Sounds*								
K	ka カ	ki キ	ku ク	ke ケ	ko コ	→	ga ガ	gı ギ	gu グ	ge ゲ	go ゴ
S	sa サ	si (shi) シ	su ス	se セ	so ソ	→	za ザ	zi (ji) ジ	zu ヅ	ze ゼ	zo ゾ
T	ta タ	ti (chi) チ	tu (tsu) ツ	te テ	to ト	→	da ダ	zi (ji) ヂ	zu ズ	de デ	do ド
N	na ナ	ni ニ	nu ヌ	ne ネ	'no ノ		ba バ	bi・ビ	bu ブ	be ベ	bo ボ
H	ha ハ	hi ヒ	hu (fu) フ	he ヘ	ho ホ		va バ	vi ビ	vu ブ	ve ベ	vo ボ
M	ma マ	mi ミ	mu ム	me メ	mo モ		pa パ	pi ピ	pu プ	pe ペ	po ポ
Y	ya ヤ		yu ユ		yo ヨ						
R	ra ラ	ri リ	ru ル	re レ	ro ロ						
W	wa ワ	(w)i ヰ		(w)e ヱ	(w)o ヲ						
N	final ン		V initial ヴ								

	Long Vowels				
	(Follow the romanization except usually for				
	oo and for all words of foreign origin)				
aa	アア	kaa˙ カア	baa	バア etc.	
ii	イイ	tii チイ	mii	ミイ etc.	but アー, キー, スー etc. in foreign words
uu	ウウ	guu グウ	suu	スウ etc.	
ee	エエ	nee ネエ	mee	メエ etc.	
oo	オウ	koo コウ	too	トウ etc. (but	
	オオ and コオ and トオ in *ooi* "many," *oo-* "big," *koori* "ice," *tooru* "to pass along" and related words).				

Diphthongs					
Short Vowels (*ki* etc. + *ya*, *yu* or *yo*)			Long Vowels		
			Japanese Words (Add single vowel)		Foreign Words (Add — [or ⏐])
kya キャ	*tya* チャ	etc.	*zyaa* ジャア· etc.		*tyaa* チャー etc.
zyu ジュ	*myu* ミュ	etc.	*kyuu* キュウ etc.		*zyuu* ジュー etc.
she シェ	*che* チェ	etc.			*shee* シェー etc.
kyo キョ	*ryo* リョ	etc.	*tyoo* チョオ etc.		*syoo* ショー etc.

Miscellaneous Uses in Foreign Words									
F: *fa*	ファ	*fi*	フィ	*fu*	フ	*fe*	フェ	*fo*	フォ
V: *va*	{ バ / ヴァ	*vi*	{ ビ / ヴィ	*vu*	{ ブ / ヴゥ	*ve*	{ ベ / ヴェ	*vo*	{ ボ / ヴォ
J: *je*	{ ジェ / ゼ								

Appendix 5
PRINTED FORMS OF KANA

	A あ ア	I い イ	U う ウ	E え エ	O お オ
K	*ka* か カ	*ki* き キ	*ku* く ク	*ke* け ケ	*ko* こ コ
S	*sa* さ サ	*si (shi)* し シ	*su* す ス	*se* せ セ	*so* そ ソ
T	*ta* た タ	*ti (chi)* ち チ	*tu (tsu)* つ ツ	*te* て テ	*to* と ト
N	*na* な ナ	*ni* に ニ	*nu* ぬ ヌ	*ne* ね ネ	*no* の ノ
H	*ha* は ハ	*hi* ひ ヒ	*hu (fu)* ふ フ	*he* へ ヘ	*ho* ほ ホ
M	*ma* ま マ	*mi* み ミ	*mu* む ム	*me* め メ	*mo* も モ
Y	*ya* や ヤ		*yu* ゆ ユ		*yo* よ ヨ
R	*ra* ら ラ	*ri* り リ	*ru* る ル	*re* れ レ	*ro* ろ ロ
W	*wa* わ ワ	*(w)i* ゐ ヰ		*(w)e* ゑ ヱ	*(w)o* を ヲ
N	final ん ン				

(Shown below are printed forms of the Final Test sentences in Appendix 2.)

1. あなたのともだちはまだアメリカにいますか。

2. いえ、もうヨーロッパへりょこうしています。

3. わたしのはこのなかになにかはいっていますか。

4. え、レター・ペーパーもペンもインキもはいっています。

5. あそこでタイプライターをつかっているのはねえさんでしょう。

6. ぎんざのスポーツのみせでゆみとやをちゅうもんしてきました。

7. あそこになにがありますか。いすとテーブルがあります。

8. いすはいくつありますか。よっつあります。

9. テーブルはいくつありますか。ふたつあります。

10. そこにフォークがいくつありますか。むっつあります。

11. ナイフもむっつありますか。ナイフはななつあります。